THE
MARKETING
INSTITUTE

This book is the product of a competition sponsored by The Marketing Institute and run in association with the Irish Marketing Teachers Association.

The adjudicators for the competition were: Anthony C. Cunningham, James J. Ward and Catherine KilBride.

Irish Studies in Management

Irish Studies in Management is a series of texts and research-based monographs covering management and business studies. Published by Oak Tree Press in association with the Graduate School of Business at University College Dublin, the series aims to publish significant contributions to the study of management and business in Ireland, especially where they address issues of major relevance to Irish management in the context of international developments, particularly within the European Union. Mindful that most texts and studies in current use in Irish business education take little direct account of Irish or European conditions, the series seeks to make available to the specialist and general reader works of high quality which comprehend issues and concerns arising from the practice of management and business in Ireland. The series aims to cover subjects ranging from management, accountancy, marketing, economics, industrial relations/human resource management and international business. Studies of public policy and public affairs of relevance to business and economic life will also be published in the series.

CASE STUDIES IN MARKETING

Edited by
Anthony C. Cunningham,
James J. Ward and Catherine KilBride

Oak Tree Press
Dublin
in association with
Graduate School of Business
University College Dublin

Oak Tree Press
Merrion Building
Lower Merrion Street
Dublin 2, Ireland

A catalogue record of this book is
available from the British Library

ISBN 1-86076-013-9

Printed in Ireland by Colour Books Ltd.

Contents

About the Contributors

Seán de Burca lectures in International Marketing and Business-to-Business Marketing at University College Dublin. He has lectured on MBA programmes in France, Hungary and Romania. His main research interest and consultancy work have focused on how firms internationalise from a network perspective.

John Fahy is a Lecturer in Strategic Marketing at the University of Dublin, Trinity College. He has also been a Visiting Professor of International Management at Senshu University in Tokyo. His research interests are in the areas of global competition, business strategy and international marketing.

Alex Gibson is a Lecturer at the Dublin Institute of Technology, Cathal Brugha Street, where he teaches marketing on programmes in hotel management, rural tourism and tourism marketing. He has published in the area of tourism education and rural tourism marketing and has acted as an advisor on tourism projects in Ireland, Argentina, the Czech Republic and Romania.

Maeve McArdle is a Lecturer in Management and Marketing at Dundalk Regional Technical College. She has been involved in the establishment of more than thirty small businesses in Dundalk, and in 1993 compiled a book on funding sources for businesses in Ireland.

Gerry Mortimer is a Senior Lecturer in Marketing at the Dublin Institute of Technology in Mountjoy Square. He is the author of several case studies and also works extensively as a consultant to Irish industry and development agencies.

Barra O Cinneide is Professor of Marketing and Course Leader of the Agribusiness Programme at the University of Limerick. His research interests include analysis of Irish sectoral development, including the effects on agriculture and tourism following Ireland's membership of the EC, and emergent indigenous enterprises — the subject of over 80 published case studies since 1979.

Elizabeth Reynolds lectures in the Department of Marketing at University College Dublin, where she specialises in food marketing, international marketing and competititive marketing strategies. Prior to joining UCD, she held a number of senior marketing positions in the food, beverage and healthcare industries.

Ann Torres is a Lecturer in Marketing at University College Galway. She received her MBA from the University of California and is currently carrying out research on entrepreneurship and enterprise development. Her other areas of interest are promotion management, information technology and marketing and strategic marketing.

INTRODUCTION

For the second time, we as marketing instructors must express our appreciation to The Marketing Institute for facilitating the publication of this collection of Irish marketing case studies.

The 1992 Irish Marketing Teachers' Association (IMTA) Conference in Galway, where the idea for such a venture found its genesis on a delightfully sunny day in May, is to be recorded with grateful appreciation.

The Irish marketing classroom has been well served by international case studies. However, we are all acutely aware that good local contemporary teaching cases are very scarce. Case writing is a highly skilled process, the output of which has a short shelf life. Consequently, to maintain a steady stream of *good* cases is both difficult and expensive.

As adjudicators for this second volume, we were faced with several difficulties — as well as several delights! On commencing the process it soon became evident that a significant learning process had occurred since the first volume of Irish cases written by members of the IMTA was published by the Institute in 1993. The case writers had clearly taken on board the lessons learned from the first effort.

ROLE OF CASE STUDIES

As adjudicators we have tried to make clear our understanding of the role of case studies in the classroom. We believe that case studies are a powerful learning tool in the enhancement of the diagnostic skills necessary for successful; management practice. It is no accident that they have been borrowed and adapted by the business schools from medical education where they are used for a similar purpose, that is, improving the diagnostic skills of medical practitioners.

Case studies are *not* the same as case histories. Case histories have their place in the education process, but the learning objective is quite different.

CRITERIA USED IN JUDGING CASES

In inviting entries to this year's competition only two criteria were specified for cases. These were that (a) they be Irish and (b) they should be accompanied by a teaching note.

As the purpose of the competition is to generate Irish teaching material, the first point is obviously a prerequisite.

The inclusion of a teaching note (TN) with each case gave us an essential insight to the authors' thinking on the use of the case and on its potential as a teaching tool. For the best entries we found the TNs were an important component of the total package and the quality of the notes in themselves was a useful differentiator.

WHAT WE LOOKED FOR IN CASES

1. Structure, Presentation and Narrative

The best cases were well-crafted stories which were interesting to read, well written, clearly structured and immediately excited an interest to use them. They had an opening which put the reader in the picture quickly, and had "read through" strength. The exhibits and data provided had a purpose and were well presented.

2. Case Focus

A good case may focus on one problem or many. It should be possible, having read the case, to write a clear paragraph outlining the main issues in it. Our preference was for cases that were "issue-rich".

A balance should be struck between explicit problem definition in the case and the need to let the students discover issues for themselves. In this respect, the TNs should provide the reader with the information regarding problems/issues to be investigated. Clearly the complexity level here will be related to the target student group, which again the TN should specify.

3. Analytical Opportunities

We particularly liked cases which presented issues, facts and data which required students to undertake various forms of analysis. These could include linking data, extrapolating, correlating, doing ratio analysis, forecasting, analysis of sales data, SWOT analysis, application of analytical marketing techniques or models.

4. Decision-making

Arising out of the analysis we also looked for areas where decisions were called for. Case teaching is designed to provide training for students in decision-making so an essential element in a case should be the need to make clear decisions and to show how to implement them.

5. Opportunities to Demonstrate Marketing Principles

Cases should provide opportunities for the teacher to apply marketing principles, theories, models, etc. These serve to reinforce other aspects of marketing programmes.

6. Relevance to Current Issues

Two aspects here that we liked in cases were:

1. Opportunities to discuss current trends in marketing practice, new developments and changes in the "real world" as demonstrated in cases, and

2. A focus on current trends in various environmental areas. Students like cases to be current and they like to identify with the situation in a case. While this may shorten a case's useful life, it also has benefits in terms of student identification with situations.

Finally, we do appreciate well-proofed copy lacking in elementary errors, and data which is presented with sources clearly identified.

COURSE DESIGN

The portfolio of cases in this publication can be incorporated into course design in many ways. The following brief description of the cases may be of help in such a task.

1. **Recyclights Inc**. This case by Ann Torres (UCG) is about the establishment of a new venture in Ireland which recycles products containing mercury, principally fluorescent lights. It could be used as a vehicle to help students understand the complexities of start-up and new venture issues.

2. **Firehouse Technologies Ltd**. A delightful case by Gerry Mortimer (DIT, Mountjoy Square) in new product development is ideal for a course in enterprise development. It traces the development of a new product (equipment for winding and washing fire hoses) up to and including a trial purchase which ends in failure. Those with an entrepreneurial trait will empathise!

3. **Northern Ireland Tourist Board**. This case by Maeve McArdle (Dundalk RTC) has a particularly topical dimension, given the current pace of the peace process and the need for students to appreciate some of the macro marketing implications of cross-border development. It can be used to cover such topics as competitive strategy, product development and marketing research in a critical service sector of the economy.

4. **North Clare LEADER Tourism Promotions**. This case by Alex Gibson (DIT, Cathal Brugha Street) nicely complements the Northern Ireland Tourist Board one as it focuses on a micro-level tourism initiative similar to many being undertaken locally across the country. It also covers such contemporary issues as co-operative marketing (strategic alliances), and societally responsible marketing (sustainable tourism). A video is also available to accompany this case.

5. **Mitsubishi Electric Ireland Ltd**. This runner-up case by John Fahy (TCD) is an excellent one to give students an awareness of the need to be able to manage change in the distribution channel. The growth of retailer power in the food and hardware/DIY sectors is highly visible. A similar pattern is developing in consumer electronics. Developing successful strategies to cope with such changes is the thrust of the case.

6. **Monaghan Mushrooms**. This case by Barra O Cinneide (University of Limerick), which concerns a highly successful

enterprise in the Irish horticultural sector, provides a platform for discussing many issues in marketing and business strategy. Strategic issues which can be covered include technology investment, acquisition and diversification options, and market development both domestic and international.

7. **Rockers for Walkers by Cherokee**. This winning case is another written by Gerry Mortimer (DIT, Mountjoy Square). It concerns a new product launch by a small Irish footwear company in a rapidly changing but relatively mature industry and raises numerous issues of how an SME copes with change through technology transfer — the launch on the Irish market of a radically new type of shoe already available on the US market. It provides the case instructor with several case discussion options.

8. **Moffett Engineering**. This runner-up case written by Elizabeth Reynolds and Sean de Burca (UCD) focuses on international marketing strategy. It provides an excellent vehicle on which to pursue many of the issues of internationalisation faced by Irish SMEs, and a particularly good platform to illustrate how strategic options open to the firm in international markets have a profound influence on market strategies.

It must be stated that in our opinion the standard achieved in the 1995 case writing exercise reflects great credit on the authors. We trust you will enjoy reading these cases as much as we did.

Anthony C. Cunningham
Professor of Marketing, UCD

James Ward
Professor of Marketing, UCG

Catherine KilBride
Director of Education, MII

1

RECYCLIGHTS INC.:[1] ENVIRONMENTAL PROTECTION THROUGH MERCURY RECLAMATION™

Ann M. Torres

INTRODUCTION

"The price of a healthy environment is eternal vigilance." — Mitra

Concern for the environment is a societal market trend that has inspired new industries. "Recyclights™" is one firm that has benefited from this trend. As their name suggests, the firm recycles lights, principally fluorescent and high intensity discharge (HID) lamps. These types of lamps contain mercury and the danger is that they can leak mercury (as well as heavy metals like lead and cadmium), when broken in landfills or burned in incinerators. On average, a 4-foot fluorescent bulb contains 35 to 75 mgs. of mercury. This is a relatively small amount, yet, fifteen, 4-foot fluorescent lamps contain enough mercury to contaminate an average sized lake for several hundred years.

Recyclights' provides a unique service in that it avails of a reverse manufacturing process that successfully converts hazardous waste into non-hazardous waste. As a result, fluorescent and HID lights are rendered into glass and metal powder, and liquid mercury. In these forms, virtually 100 per cent of the raw materials of standard fluorescent lights can be re-used in the production of

---

[1] This case was prepared by Ann M. Torres, Lecturer in Marketing at University College Galway. It is intended to be used as a basis for class discussion rather than to illustrate either effective or in effective handling of a business situation. The case is based on a real-life situation, no figures have been disguised.

other products. An additional benefit is that Recyclights provides to each client a certificate of conversion (i.e. that mercury from the lamps has been reclaimed), thus eliminating the possibility of any future liability.

COMPANY BACKGROUND

Recyclights was founded in April 1992 by Keith Thorndyke, in Minneapolis, Minnesota, USA. Mr. Thorndyke was a recent graduate in Business and Entrepreneurship from the University of St. Thomas, Minneapolis at the time he had the idea for his business. Due to legislation passed in Minnesota in 1992, "generators", or users of lamps, were no longer allowed to dispose of them without first removing the mercury. Recyclights was formed to process fluorescent and HID lamps which have come under regulation by state and local authorities. The firm purchased equipment from Sweden which processes the lamps and reclaims the mercury. This is presently one of the few machines of its kind in the United States, and Recyclights has exclusive geographic rights to the states bordering Minnesota (i.e. Iowa, Illinois, Wisconsin, North and South Dakota.) Beginning in 1994, Recyclights attained exclusive geographic rights to the states of Illinois, Indiana, Michigan, Ohio and Kentucky. In just two years of operation, Recyclights has become profitable with sales nearing $2 million in 1994.

MARKET OPPORTUNITIES

Recyclights is actively seeking to expand its business. The opportunity for new markets is an important issue as life cycles are short (i.e. continued reclamation of one type of product in one geographic region is limited) Recyclights is looking at managing other items which contain mercury such as batteries (i.e. car, transistor, household etc.) Not only are they seeking other items for reclamation of mercurial wastes, they are also investigating other geographic sites. The firm has already expanded its operations to Tallahassee, Florida in August 1994, and intends to target other markets where governmental regulation requires that these lamps be processed before disposal (e.g. California, Michigan, Wisconsin, Indiana, Massachusetts).

Another potential market is Europe. Ms Mary Riebe Cary, a marketing consultant who had been involved in the formation and development of Recyclights, has specifically identified Ireland as a possible site for operations. Her interest in the Irish market came about during a visit to Ireland in January 1994 where she noticed a fluorescent light sticking out of a bin. Since this visit Ms Cary has been researching recycling in Ireland, legislation governing the disposal of toxic waste, as well as present usage and handling of lights containing mercury.

Ms Cary views Ireland as a desirable location because its population correlates with the population in Minnesota and because Ireland relies almost exclusively on landfill waste disposal. Furthermore, recycling as an industry in Ireland is at the introductory stage. Present legislation in Ireland prohibits the disposal of hazardous waste in landfills, but enforcement and compliance are nonexistent. Ms Cary pointed out that a window of opportunity exists for business development and growth potential within Ireland and Europe. However, Recyclights is not interested in pursuing the European market, as the firm is already targeting a number of new markets in the United States and does not have sufficient resources to pursue markets within Europe as well.

Having conducted the initial market research on Ireland, Ms Cary is firmly convinced of its market potential. As a result, she has negotiated with Recyclights to agree to sell their equipment and offer any consulting which would be necessary. Recyclights has made it clear that they are not interested in a joint venture or a licensing agreement and that they do not want to be involved in the business, although they are interested in selling their equipment. Ms Cary believes that the formation of this new company in Ireland would have the benefits of Recyclights' expertise, yet be able to develop the business in Ireland and carry the rights to the rest of Europe.

Ms Cary moved to Ireland in September, 1994 to conduct further research and to develop the plans for the new venture. Her main concerns are whether she will be able to acquire sufficient financial support from various governmental and trade bodies within Ireland for her start-up operation and a verification of market size. If her operation were to get off the ground, she would require a 5,000 square foot facility which would eventually employ 15 to 20 people. Aware that job creation is an important issue in acquiring governmental support, particularly in the area of grants and tax relief, Ms Cary is concerned whether her initially small operation would be of interest. However, she recognises that supplemental businesses, such as transporters which would haul the lights for recycling, and companies which might use the reclaimed glass, metal and liquid mercury in their production operations, would also benefit. This is just one of the issues that Ms Cary is considering.

It is January, 1995 and she is at the stage of her research where she is ready to plan her strategy. She realises that selling and marketing her idea to a variety of publics is an important key to the success of the new venture. The following pages are a summary of her research findings.

MERCURY

> "It is the hottest, the coldest, a true healer, a wicked murderer, a precious medicine, and a deadly poison, a friend that can flatter and lie" — John Woodall, Military Surgeon, 1642.

Mercury, or "quicksilver" in keeping with its elusive nature, is an element which is considered to be ubiquitous throughout nature. High contents of mercury have been identified on the earth's surface and under the seas. Mercury forms hundreds of compounds. The most common type of naturally-occurring mercury is found in the form of the sulfide cinnabar, which is present in at least 30 different minerals.

Mercury Contamination

> "Mercury is a unique pollutant because of its apparent indestructibility." — Mitra

Environmental Protection Agency (EPA) studies in the United States show that only a teaspoon of mercury can contaminate a lake for hundreds of years. Once mercury enters the aquatic food chain, at each trophic level, less mercury is excreted than is ingested. Thus, there is proportionately more mercury in algae than in the water in which they live, more mercury in fish that feed upon the algae than in the algae itself, etc. Essentially, the rate at which mercury is eliminated from the muscle tissue is less than its incorporation. This is how mercury may accumulate in algae, fish and humans.

Bacteria and decay promote the conversion of any mercury into methyl-mercury. All forms of mercury introduced into the aquatic environment can be converted into methyl-mercury. Almost all (i.e. 98 per cent) of mercury found in animal tissues is in the form of methyl-mercury. Data from rats and humans indicate that more than 90 per cent of methyl-mercury in food is absorbed. The implications of mercury poisoning in humans are documented in the Japanese incident which occurred in 1953 and is known as "Minamata Disease."

Minamata is a Japanese fishing village located near the effluent of a large factory which used mercury in the manufacture of plastic. The mercury from the manufacturing process entered the plant's effluent which in turn flowed into the sea. The epidemic of poisoning in Minamata was traced to the consumption of fish contaminated by the plant's effluent. The mercury contamination caused a host of neurological damage, such as memory loss, paralysis and movement disorders, and in severe cases the loss of all muscular control.

Monitoring of and Standards for Mercury Concentration

The ubiquity of mercury means that all humans will absorb a certain amount of the element from food, water and air. However, too much mercury is toxic to all organic matter. This points to the need for monitoring the environment and establishing standards for the presence of mercury at appropriate levels. Environmental standards for mercury may be defined in a number of ways. The suggested standards are as follows:

- The suggested level for atmospheric mercury is 0.005 mg/m^3 (i.e. micrograms per cubed metre), with an upper limit of 0.1 mg/m^3.
- In the working environment, atmospheric mercury levels are recommended not to exceed 0.025 mg/m^3.

- For drinking water it is 0.005 ug/l (i.e. micrograms per litre) for mercury or mercuric ions which is equivalent to 5.0 parts per thousand millions, with an upper limit of 1.0 ug/l. Note that it is not until the levels of mercury exceed 1.0 micrograms per litre that it is extracted from drinking water.
- Acceptable levels of mercury for fishery waters is 2.0 ug/l with an upper limit of 3.0 ug/l.
- For food, principally fish flesh, the upper limit is 0.4 to 0.5 ppm (i.e. parts per million — wet weight.)

Within Ireland, accepted levels of mercury are governed by "good manufacturing practice" which closely follows the standards listed above. Irish standards have not yet been incorporated into legislation. This is due in part to the fact that the Irish EPA is only a year old and has not yet addressed this issue. Also, under "scientific co-operation", various EU committees will be discussing standards for mercury and other toxic substances in the coming year. It is presumed that the Irish EPA will adopt the EU standards.

In 1986, Forbairt[2] conducted a water quality study for Ireland in which mercury concentrations were screened at various water station locations. The average level of mercury concentration was 0.2 ug/1 (micrograms per litre). Forbairt's report indicated that this was considered to be an adequate abstraction for water assessment. Although median levels of mercury concentration were below the average of 0.2 ug/1, the average concentration level was four times the recommended level for fishery water of 0.005 ug/1. Furthermore, with the exception of the Suir and the Boyne rivers, there were a small number of samples from each river which had mercury concentrations above the screening level of 0.2 ug/1. The highest value of 0.9 ug/1 was recorded for the Avoca river. It is not clear whether such values reflect natural variations or indicate

[2] Forbairt was established by the Irish Government on the 1st of January, 1994 when EOLAS and the IDA came together. As such, the 1986 water quality study was conducted by EOLAS, which is now part of Forbairt. Forbairt's mission is to facilitate the development of Irish Industry, to encourage technological innovation and to provide technology based services to all types of firms

significant contamination by artificial sources. Forbairt recommended that in view of the recommended concentration level, there is a need for further clarification of the significance of these relatively high values and for continued monitoring.

EC REGULATIONS ON HAZARDOUS WASTE

The European Commission considers that toxic and dangerous wastes represent one of the greatest environmental protection problems in the European Community as a whole, there is a deficiency of 50 per cent in capacity for their safe disposal. It is essential to know of the presence and movement of hazardous wastes and to ensure they are disposed of in a controlled way.

The European Community has two sets of regulations[3] and one Council Directive which govern the disposal of hazardous waste:

- 1979, General Waste Regulations (S.I. No. 390 of 1979)
- 1982, Toxic and Dangerous Waste Regulations (S.I. No. 33 of 1982)
- 1991, Council Directive on Hazardous Waste (91/689/EEC).

Ireland has adopted both of the regulations and the directive. The 1982, Toxic and Dangerous Waste Regulations list mercury and mercury compounds as a toxic substance selected as requiring priority considerations. Under these regulations, Member States are required to do the following:

- To take the appropriate measures to encourage, as a matter of priority, the *prevention* of toxic and dangerous waste, its *processing and recycling*, *the extraction of raw materials* and possibly energy therefrom and other processes for the *re-use* of such waste.

---

[3] It is worthy to note that an EC Regulation is binding in its entirety and directly applicable in all the member countries. This differs from an EC Directive which is binding as to the result to be achieved, but not as to the means to be adopted. With an EC Directive, it is left to each member state to decide how to achieve that result.

- To take the necessary measures to ensure that toxic and dangerous waste is *disposed of without endangering human health and without harming the environment*.
- To take the necessary steps to *prohibit the abandonment and uncontrolled discharge, binning or carriage* of toxic and dangerous waste as well as its consignment to installations, establishments, or undertakings other than those which are permitted to do so.
- Installations, establishments, or undertakings which carry out the storage, treatment and/or deposit of toxic and dangerous waste *must obtain a permit* from the competent authorities of the Member States.

ENVIRONMENTAL LAW

The best environmental policy prevents pollution at the source rather than counteract the effects after the damage. In this respect, *environmental law* strives to offer protection *before* the damage is done. This differs from *common law* which gives protection after the damage is done.

Almost all municipal refuse and industrial waste are disposed of by landfill in Ireland, although Ireland's national waste disposal strategy does call for improved arrangements for the disposal of hazardous wastes which are not suitable for landfilling. Currently, many of the landfill sites are older and do not have the appropriate processes to dispose of hazardous waste properly. As such, Ireland is currently in violation of the prescribed EC regulations and it is possible that a case could be brought under the auspices of environmental law.

Furthermore, some of these older landfill sites are located dangerously close to water sources. The protection of water resources is very important and, as such, a satisfactory landfill site must either contain the leachate within the site, after which it must be captured and treated, or allow the leachate to migrate slowly and in a predictable manner so it is naturally attenuated to a relatively harmless liquid before it enters aquifers or streams.

Ireland's Fisheries Act and Water Pollution Act provide legislative protection for water resources. The Fisheries Act prohibits any substance from entering waterways which is liable to enter fish or spawning grounds and which is likely to injure fish. Under this act it is not necessary to show any injury, merely that the substance is liable to cause injury.

Furthermore, the presence of this substance will also be considered water pollution if the substance were discharged into water resources for domestic, industrial and recreational use. Note that actual water pollution need not occur. It is sufficient to show that the presence of this substance has the potential to cause pollution and damage. It is also worthy to note that anyone can take an action under the Water Pollution and Fisheries Acts. It is curious that there have not been a number of such cases presented in the courts (and in the media). However, this may be due in part to the lack of education of the general public, government, fishing industry and other special interest groups on the impact of mercurial poisoning.

IRISH LEGISLATION AND RECYCLING

Efforts made to protect the environment are relatively new in Ireland, although great strides have been made in the last few years. The Environmental Protection Agency (EPA) of Ireland was established on January 1st, 1994. In that same year, on the 28th of July, the Department of the Environment (DOE) and the Environmental Protection Agency (EPA) launched "Recycling for Ireland." This is a strategy document which outlines the efforts Ireland intends to implement to reduce waste and to manage waste disposal in a more environmentally friendly manner.

The creation of this document was in response to the increasing problem of waste and its disposal. Municipal waste in the European Union as a whole has grown by 13 per cent in 5 years. On average, each person in the EU is responsible for creating 0.7 to 0.8 kg of waste per person per day. The average for Ireland is higher than this, at 0.96 kg per person per day.

With the increasing number of landfill sites closing throughout Ireland, the need to address the waste issue is becoming more pressing. For example, Counties Wicklow and Kerry are currently looking for suitable locations for new landfill operations. In County Galway, landfill sites in Ballinasloe and Headford will be full to capacity by the end of the 1995. Essentially, waste space in the form of landfill sites is depleting. New landfill sites will have to be developed according to more stringent requirements for design and construction together with the stricter day-to-day operational controls. These requirements derive from a draft EU Directive on Landfill, from provisions of the EPA Act, 1992 and from the forthcoming Waste Bill. Typical costs of disposing of domestic and commercial wastes to landfill are now in the range of £5 to £7 per tonne. However, as a result of these stiffer regulations, these costs will substantially increase.

Until recently, recycling may have been seen as a fringe activity undertaken mainly by voluntary organisations. The EPA and the DOE, in working towards waste reduction, are encouraging County Councils, commercial businesses and households to subscribe to a "hierarchy of waste" (see Figure 1). In such a hierarchy, prevention is the first strategy to employ in addressing the issue of waste and disposal in landfill is the last.

FIGURE 1: HIERARCHY OF WASTE

1. Prevention
2. Reduction
3. Recycling
4. Treatment
5. Disposal

Ireland recycles relatively little of the waste it creates. Only 7.4 per cent of the total waste from Irish households and commercial enterprises is recycled. This is well below the European average, which is estimated to be in the range of 15 to 20 per cent. Of the 7.4 per cent that is recycled, the majority is done by the commercial sector. Irish households recycle less than 2 per cent (i.e. 1.4 per cent) of the waste they create. Tables 1 and 2 outline in greater detail the household and commercial waste figures for Ireland in 1993.

TABLE 1: HOUSEHOLD AND COMMERCIAL WASTE IN IRELAND, 1993 — QUANTITIES ARISING AND RECYCLED

Material	*Quantities Arising (tonnes)*	*Quantities Landfilled (tonnes)*	*Quantities Recycled (tonnes)*	*Recycling Rate (%)*
Paper	381,764	308,369	73,400	19.2
Glass	107,325	85,325	22,000	20.5
Plastic	140,850	140,750	100	neg
Metals*	68,573	51,978	16,595	24.2
Textiles	83,555	71,555	12,000	14.4
Organic	572,971	572,951	20	neg
Other	323,656	3232,656	0	0
Total	1,678,699	1,554,584	124,115	7.4

* Metals includes ferrous and nonferrous metals and aluminium

Source: Ireland's Department of Environment

TABLE 2: HOUSEHOLD WASTE IN IRELAND, 1993 — QUANTITIES ARISING AND RECYCLED

Material	*Quantities Arising (tonnes)*	*Quantities Landfilled (tonnes)*	*Quantities Recycled (tonnes)*	*Recycling Rate (%)*
Paper	140,190	137,777	2,413	1.7
Glass	55,958	45,958	10,000	17.9
Plastic	104,763	104,663	100	0.1
Metals*	32,945	32,295	650	2.0
Textiles	71,574	71,554	20	-
Organic	379,415	379,395	20	-
Other	126,820	126,820	-	-
Total	911,665	898,462	13,203	1.4

* Metals includes ferrous and nonferrous metals and aluminium

Source: Ireland's Department of Environment

IRELAND'S WASTE BILL

Under the new Operational Programme for Environmental Services, some £30 million investment in recycling infrastructure will be EU co-financed during the period of the recycling strategy. About 10 per cent of those funds will address the specific requirements for hazardous waste recovery. Such capital investment will provide more widespread, accessible and user friendly local authority collection and segregation systems for recycling. All major local authority landfills will also be progressively equipped with these facilities.

To support these initiatives and the existing European waste legislation, the Department of Environment intends to introduce a new waste bill by the end of 1995.[4] It will be a "general framework" bill legislating powers to be used to achieve recycling targets. The focus is on producer responsibility and awards powers to local and government authorities to intervene if necessary and to require compliance, that is, the enforcement of legislation through issuing fines for non-compliance. An outline of the principal powers of the Waste Bill are listed below:

- Producers or distributors will be required to take back used products/packaging or arrange for their collection and recovery.
- Producers, retailers and distributors will be required to operate deposit and refund schemes for specified products.[5]
- Manufacturers will be required to use a proportion of recycled materials.
- There will be restrictions on the use of specified materials and/or financial instruments in support of recycling (i.e. EU co-financing and other financial incentives to aid recycling efforts.)
- Product labelling will be required to indicate recyclability, recycled content etc.

Waste management is emerging in all countries as a symbol of the sustainable approach to consumption. The reasons to recycle include the conservation of resources, landfill and energy. Emphasis

---

[4] The Irish Waste Bill will not become law until 6-12 months after it is put before the Dáil.

[5] As of the writing of this case, no particular material has yet been specified as a "product". Although, it is expected that the same substances named in the 1982 Toxic and Dangerous Waste Act, one of which is mercury, will also be identified in the proposed Waste Bill.

on recycling will also favour prevention and re-use. However, there are certain myths about recycling which still prevail, such as:

- Recycling will eliminate landfill
- Everything is recyclable
- Recycling is cheap, and
- Public support is automatic.

Successful promotion of recycling will depend significantly on the attitudes, behaviour and influence of the public, and compliance with the law. The active support and participation of the public must be encouraged and facilitated by the promotion of awareness and accurate information about products, materials and waste.

LAMP RECYCLING

Lamp recycling in the United States developed as a result of state and federal regulation which prohibit the disposal of hazardous waste in landfills due to the leaching of toxic substances into soil and water, and which require environmentally sound processes to handle toxic substances. Fluorescent lights and HID lamps contain mercury and as such are classified as hazardous waste. This type of environmental legislation provided the main impetus for Recyclights' incorporation in 1992.

Recyclights' means of differentiation from other lamp recyclers are two-fold: (1) all the parts from the lamps are converted into saleable materials after processing; and (2) the certificate of reclamation which verifies that the mercury from the lamps has been properly extracted. Such certification eliminates future liability concerns and future handling of mercury. Thus, it is the larger firms, and their refuse operators, which are more likely to take the initiative to avail of this service so as to avoid liability. It is expected that with stricter EC directives and regulations that a similar situation will evolve in Europe.

EQUIPMENT AND TECHNOLOGY

Recycling technology currently offers four types of mercury reclamation processing: wet crushing, dry crushing, shredding/washing, and de-manufacture. A description of each process follows:

- **Wet Crushing:** Lamps are added to a polysulfide solution in a tank and crushed. The solution is pumped back into a container and crushate vacuumed into a transfer container which is drained and dumped into a container for shipping to another location.
- **Dry Crushing:** Crushate is collected in a filter container. These filters are deemed hazardous and an outside source is required for the deposit and handling of these filters.
- **Shredding/Washing:** Mercury is stripped over active carbon filters and these filters are then shipped to an outside supplier dealing in hazardous waste.
- **De-Manufacture:** Mercury is reclaimed as well as other materials existing in the system, all of which may be recycled for use in the production of other products.

After analysing the world marketplace, Recyclights determined that a firm in Karlskrona, Sweden, MRT Systems, offered the best equipment for the process of *de-manufacture*. MRT's technology was developed in 1975 when the Swedish EPA decided to do something about Mercury pollution. As the lamp manufacturing industry is the biggest mercury polluter, the Swedish lamp manufacturers developed the process that is now the MRT system. The rights were purchased when MRT was founded in 1980.

Since 1980 MRT has been marketing its technology, which vaporises the mercury, oxidises the organic particles in an afterburner, then condenses the mercury into cooling traps. The entire process which separates mercury from glass, light sources, batteries and dental amalgam, takes from eight to twenty hours depending upon whether the items are treated beforehand. Pretreatment technologies marketed by MRT include an end cutting machine for fluorescent lights, which vacuums mercury from inside the glass tubing, and a crusher/sieving machine that can handle 4,000 fluorescent tubes an hour. The company markets two types of distillers, one for fluorescent lights and other sources with low quantities of mercury, and a second for handling products with larger quantities of mercury such as batteries.

Recyclights required two main pieces of equipment, a crush and sieve (costing $700,000) and a standard distiller (costing $150,000). MRT equipment has a capacity exceeding 21 million lamps per year. In using the equipment, Recyclights discovered that the crush and sieve were designed to handle a volume far beyond the present and anticipated demand of Recyclights. In response, Recyclights developed a new crush and sieve product which is in operation in their new location in Tallahassee, Florida. Although many of the key features presently remain proprietary, the equipment is designed to handle a smaller volume of lights. Recyclights will sell their equipment for substantially less than what MRT charges for its equipment.

COMPETITION

In the United States, competition at the moment is growing, as other firms perceive the emerging opportunity. Recyclights began its business in Minnesota with two competitors already present in the market. In Ireland, there are two firms which have been identified as being in direct competition with Ms Cary's new venture. One company, Greenstar Recycling Ltd. in Dublin, provides a waste management programme for various companies. For £10, Greenstar rents to each client a container which will hold about 100 fluorescent tubes. The fee upon collection of a container is £50. Greenstar uses machinery which crushes the lamps under water (i.e. wet crushing) and the waste is then sent for disposal.

The other competitor, Irish Lamp Disposable Company in Co. Kildare, will collect fluorescent lights from their clients. The minimum amount for collection is 100 lamps and the charge is £1 per tube. The firm does not provide any container to hold the tubes while awaiting collection and the firm usually asks their clients to tape them together in bundles of 10 or 20. Upon collection, Irish Lamp provides their clients with a copy of the 1982 Toxic Waste Legislation which specifically prohibits the improper disposal of mercury. Irish Lamp uses the "Lampcracker" machine (i.e. dry crushing) which only crushes the lamps and the firm then sends the hazardous waste filters from the machine to England or Germany for further processing and disposal.

HOW RECYCLIGHTS' PRODUCT COMPARES WITH THAT OF COMPETITORS

Unlike other technologies, the crush and sieve technology reclaims mercury and transfers all hazardous waste into saleable commodities. No hazardous waste filters need to be shipped and no by-products are dumped in landfills. This technology provides complete on-site distillation thus eliminating the need for hazardous waste storage and shipment of hazardous waste.

In addition, Recyclights is a market leader. The firm provides a three-year history of operations and expertise that would be available to the Irish venture. The learning curve for this venture can be substantially shortened by Recyclights' experience. Minnesota has one of the strictest environmental safety regulations in the United States. A complete manual is available from Recyclights on providing a safe work facility. Monitored by the Minnesota Pollution Control Agency, Recyclights presently exceeds state and federal standards for regulatory compliance. Recyclights can also provide competitive de-manufacture equipment, thus offering a more cost-effective facility.

MARKET SIZE AND POTENTIAL

In the United States, fluorescent lamps account for about 80 per cent of lamps containing mercury. The exact proportion of lamps in Ireland which contain mercury has not yet been established. However, the International Commission on Illumination reports an industry average of 2.5 fluorescent lights per person, per year. The population for the Republic of Ireland is about 3.5 million and in Northern Ireland it is about 1.5 million. Furthermore, Siemens Corporation (Germany) which owns Sylvania lights, reports that new electrical sockets are growing at only 3 per cent per year, which indicates that light replacement is a continuing trend. Finally, Ireland is in the introductory stages of recycling. These points taken together suggest that there may be a substantial market in Ireland. The predominant use for fluorescent lamps is in commercial buildings, hospitals, schools and for this reason markets are likely to be identified in and around city centres.

CUSTOMER BASE

Ms Cary believes that the customer base for her new venture may develop in a similar manner as it did for Recyclights. As a source for comparison, Recyclights' primary source of business comes from independent refuse haulers. The firm estimates that 80 per cent of the lamps processed are transported through this independent network. The refuse haulers need to have a reliable place to bring lamps containing mercury, as they need to provide *their* customers, the users of the lamps, with insurance that the lamps have been processed. The remaining 15 to 25 per cent of lamps processed come in directly from end users and governmental agencies.

There is a certain degree of seasonality in their sales. Recyclights has found that in December there tends to be a year-end "clean up" which accounts for an increase of lamps processed in December, and the slower months are January, February, and March. Schools and other educational institutions tend to replace all of their lamps during the summer months, which results in large volumes that need recycling.

"Retrofitting" or "relighting" which is the replacement of lamps through out a facility is likely to have an impact. New, more energy efficient lamps (some of which do not contain mercury) are installed and old ones removed, whether the old lamps are useable or not. Many facilities managers find it easier to replace all the lamps at once rather than one by one as they burn out.

Recyclights believes that consumers will eventually be reached with additional regulation, and most likely lamps from homes will be brought to collection points, sorted and then transported to the appropriate recycling facility. In view of this, Recyclights is working on establishing networks to facilitate this.

Another consideration, particularly for growth of the business, is that product life cycles are short. Recyclights' view is that as regulation increases growth will be achieved by expanding into other forms of mercury containers (e.g. batteries).

POSITIONING AND PRICE

Ms Cary's new venture would offer a service, as opposed to the sale of a product. In this respect, the operating expenses would comprise the bulk of expenses, and the operating profit is a key measurement. The pressure the new venture will face to become profitable will be to control operating costs and also to find a way to charge a sufficiently high price for processing each lamp.

Ms Cary has noticed that Recyclights operates in an industry which is principally driven by price competition. Currently, about 75 per cent of Recyclights' processing and recycling involves 4-foot lamps. The average price Recyclights charges its clients in the United States is $0.47, which is approximately IR£0.31, and which will probably drop to $0.34 to $0.35 as volume increases. In their market, Recyclights is priced higher, but no other firm provides the mercury reclamation and quality recycling service.

Recyclights unique point of differentiation is the certification service to verify that mercurial substances have been extracted and transformed into saleable commodities such as metal and glass powder, and liquid mercury. Furthermore, the certification eliminates the possibility of liability for customers availing of Recyclights' service. Its unique positioning is safeguarded by the fact that Recyclights has geographic exclusivity to the operation of the equipment which allows them to reclaim and dispose of mercury safely. Should Ms Cary choose to pursue a site in Ireland, she would seek a similar equipment arrangement to safeguard the new venture's position within the marketplace.

DISTRIBUTION

In terms of distribution, fluorescent lights will have to be transported, or picked up and transferred to one location for recycling and mercury reclamation. Transportation costs in Ireland are higher than the European average. This may be a disincentive for some firms as this may require a higher service price to cover the cost of distribution. However, these difficulties are likely to be overcome once legislation is enforced more stringently. Under this scenario, firms will be required to dispose of toxic substances appropriately, whatever the cost. Presently, few other options exist for safe disposal in Ireland or elsewhere.

SURVEY

Ms Cary had quite a bit of secondary information on the Irish market, but was interested in gathering more specific data pertinent to her new venture. Although she found it useful to avail of Recyclights' experience as a general model against which to compare information, she was keenly aware that Ireland would be a market with its own distinct characteristics. To address this issue, Ms Cary conducted a study to get an overview of how organisations handled the disposal of fluorescent and HID lamps. One-hundred Irish firms and organisations, selected on a stratified random basis, were interviewed over the telephone. The types of organisations selected for interview were those most likely to be heavy users of lamps as follows: large corporations, government offices, banks, airports, hotels, hostels, hospitals, ESB facilities, universities and regional technical colleges. The overall results of the survey are outlined in Exhibit 1, on the following pages.

Through the survey, Ms Cary has gained greater insight into the usage and disposal of mercury containing lamps by Irish organisations. One of the more interesting survey findings is how these organisations currently dispose of their fluorescent and HID lamps. A majority of the firms interviewed dispose of their lamps in landfill sites. Yet, a substantially high proportion of the firms indicate "high/somewhat high" interest in using a recycling firm; the primary reason being for the benefit of the environment.

However, it is the belief of the interviewers that few of the organisations realise that:

- Fluorescent and HID lamps contain mercury
- Disposing of mercury containing lamps in landfill sites is hazardous
- Their current disposal methods are in violation of EC regulations, and
- They may be liable for the potential damage and injury.

In general, the telephone interviewers believe the firms to be rather ignorant about the dangers related to inappropriate disposal of mercury containing lamps. If the organisations had been more knowledgeable, particularly with respect to EC legislation, it is the interviewers' opinion that the organisations would have refused to participate in the questionnaire knowing they are in violation of the law.

EXHIBIT 1: 1995 SURVEY RESULTS OF 100 IRISH FIRMS: THEIR USE AND DISPOSAL OF MERCURY-CONTAINING LAMPS

No. of Fluorescents Used in Facility:

0 - 0	0%
1 - 60	42%
61 - 100	11%
101 - 400	20%
401 - 1000	11%
1001 - 3000	10%
3001 - 9000	6%
	100%

No. of HIDs Used in Facility:

0 - 0	78%
1 - 60	15%
61 - 100	5%
101 - 400	2%
401 - 1000	0%
1001 - 3000	0%
3001 - 9000	0%
	100%

No. of Flourescents/HIDs Disposed of Annually:

Amount unknown	29%
1 - 60	37%
61 - 100	6%
101 - 400	14%
401 - 1000	9%
1001 - 3000	4%
3001 - 9000	1%
	100%

EXHIBIT 1 (continued)

Type of Disposal Currently Used:

Bin/Dump/Skip/Landfill	74%
Lamp Crusher	17%
Recycling Firm	4%
Don't Know	3%
Not Yet Disposed	2%
	100%

Have They Changed Their Form of Lights Recently:

Yes, to Energy Savers/Long Life Bulbs	11%
Yes, to Halo Star Lights	2%
No	87%
	100%

Are They Likely to Change Their Form of Lights in the Near Future:

Yes	3%
Maybe	1%
No	96%
	100%

Degree of Interest in a Recycling and Reclamation Service:

High Interest	27%
Somewhat High Interest	41%
Somewhat Low Interest	15%
Low Interest	17%
	100%

Primary Reason for Interest in a Recycling & Reclamation Service:

For the Benefit of the Environment	60%
Increased Convenience	10%
Creation of Jobs	1%

EXHIBIT 1 (continued)

Primary Reason for Lack of Interest:

Own Facilities/Contractor's Job	2%
Cost and Storage of Lamps	27%
	100%

If They Were to Avail of the Service What Type of Transportation Would They Require:

Use Transportation Provided by the Service	65%
Use Their own Transportation Facilities	2%
Electrical Contractor/Supplier Would Provide Transport	33%
	100%

PUBLIC RELATIONS AND PROMOTION

Given the survey findings, Ms Cary recognises that awareness and education of the public will be an important aspect to her marketing plan. To persuade the various target publics of the legal and environmental forces of the recycling service, she plans to develop a public relations programme as part of her overall promotion strategy. Her principal objective in her public relations campaign will be to influence unformed or latent opinions regarding the disposal of mercury containing products.

Ms Cary's main concern is how she should develop her PR campaign so that it educates and achieves awareness among the various publics. She is aware that environmental organisations such as Green Peace and Earth Watch rely heavily on publicity through the media to convey their messages and to educate the public. Ms Cary is considering whether she should follow a similar pattern and conduct her campaign primarily through press releases, feature articles and other forms of publicity. Regardless of the tactics she pursues, the message of her PR campaign should be consistent with the new venture's overall business and marketing plans.

Ms Cary has a number of things to consider with respect to promotion, beginning with the name and image of the firm. Furthermore, in addition to public relations, she is considering how she should promote her new venture to potential clients so that they will be inclined to avail of the service. Essentially, she needs to develop a promotional plan. She knows that Recyclights has relied on direct marketing techniques, particularly telemarketing, to reach potential customers. According to Recyclights, the response from this method has been very favourable.

In addition to the types of promotional tools to be used, Ms Cary is considering which message appeal she should pursue. She has several options available, one of which is related to the issue of liability, another which employs the use of fear, and the final one which focuses on the saleability of materials reclaimed from de-manufacture.

DILEMMA

Ms Cary is faced with a number of difficult decisions. The first is whether the Irish market is of sufficient size to support the venture. If she does pursue the new venture, she will have to decide which is the best market entry strategy to follow, as well as how to develop, price, promote, and locate the service. Most of all, she is aware that she will have to be pro-active in generating support for her venture from various publics, such as the government, environmental groups, firms and organisations, as well as the general public. How would you advise Ms Cary in making these decisions?

2

Fire Hose Technologies Ltd.: A Case Study In New Product Development[1]

Gerry Mortimer

"Well, make up you mind, are you having a drink?" Noel Dillon[2] stayed slumped in the seat in the corner of the pub, oblivious of his brother-in-law Terry Joyce standing over him.

"I can't," said Noel eventually. "I have to drive back to the ferry."

"Well one pint won't kill you," continued Terry.

"Neither will it be enough after this morning," retorted Noel.

"Come on, cheer up," said Terry, "it is not the end of the world."

"It may not be the end of your world," said Noel, "but it is pretty close to the end of mine."

"Okay," muttered Noel eventually, "I'll have a pint of stout."

"You're not in Ireland now, you're in the English midlands, although I suppose they all sell stout now," replied Terry as he made his way to the bar. "It's Beamish," he said on his return, laying the two pints on the table. "Do you want any lunch?"

"No," Noel snapped. And so, the directors of Fire Hose Technologies Ltd. found themselves sitting in a pub in a small midland town, sipping Beamish and reflecting on a morning which had begun so promisingly and had ended in disaster.

"What I can't understand," said Noel after a long silent interval, "is how it could all have turned so sour in three weeks. When I spoke to Grundy three weeks ago and made this appointment he

---

[1] This case was developed as a basis for class discussion rather than to illustrate either effective or ineffective handling of an administrative situation.

[2] Names and other non-essential information have been disguised in the case.

specifically said 'sharpen your pencils and we will do a deal when you come over', and now this."

"Well he did tell us that the reason they were not going to go ahead with the order was the recent floods and the fact that the Borsetshire Fire Service had lost £2 million worth of equipment as a result," said Terry.

"But do you believe him?" asked Noel. "After all, we have invested all our efforts in getting an order from Borsetshire. They have had the product on trial for six months now. It is a week from Christmas and we will be heading into 1995 shortly with no orders and limited contacts."

"Well," said Terry, "I'm not prepared to give up so let's review the position to date and start making some decisions pretty fast."

THE IDEA

Noel Dillon had lived all his life in a small rural town in the south east of Ireland. He was in his early thirties and had spent most of his working life driving heavy vehicles. He had had a business hauling sand and aggregate which had closed when the local quarry had ceased to operate. He had then secured a contract for refuse collection from the local council and had operated three vehicles covering a large part of the country. The contract had been withdrawn in controversial circumstances and was the subject of possible litigation in 1994.

For several years, Noel had also worked as a part-time or retained firefighter in the local fire service. In most rural areas in Ireland the fire service was staffed on a part-time basis with normally eight firefighters retained. They were paid an annual fee and were also paid for each call out. In many cases there was a family tradition of working in the fire service and, in fact, Noel's father had been the local station officer. The local brigade operated from a small building which housed the vehicle and equipment and a meeting room/office.

It was as a result of working with the fire service that Noel developed the idea for a new product. All fire tenders carried hoses. Normally vehicles carried two types of hose. On either side of the vehicle was mounted a drum on which was coiled a small diameter rubber hose which was known as the first aid reel hose. It was so called because it was usually the first hose used at an incident. It used an on-board water supply which would last up to 20 minutes and could be brought into action quickly. However, its effectiveness was limited. Each vehicle also carried up to 30 lengths of larger diameter hose. When laid flat this hose normally measured 4 inches in width. This hose had two purposes. It drew water from the nearest source of supply to the pump at the rear of the vehicle. It also carried water from the pump to the source of the fire. Most hoses were used to link the water supply to the pump. In urban areas this was normally a nearby hydrant. In rural areas it could be a lake or river. The hose was stored on the vehicle in rolls with a coupling at either end. On reaching an incident, the rolls of hose were removed from the vehicle, laid out on the ground and coupled together linking the water supply, vehicle pump and fire. The vehicle pump was driven by a PTO shaft operated by the vehicle's engine.

When the incident was over, firefighters would decouple the hose and taking one end in their hands would roll the hose along the ground and then replace the hose on the vehicle. Frequently the hose was dirty as a result of its contact with the ground and it would have to be laid out again at the station and washed. While unrolling the hose was, and was designed to be, fast and easily done, hose rolling was a difficult manual exercise involving the firefighter bending over while walking the length of the hose. When a hose had to be washed at the station the same operation had to be repeated. When rolled, one coupling was normally left in the centre of the roll and one on the outside of the roll. Some services used a form of rolling called Dutch rolling. In this case the rolling started from the mid point of the hose and, as a result, both couplings finished up on the outside of the hose. This form of rolling meant that two firefighters could each take hold of a coupling and move quickly to where the coupling was required. On the other hand it was more difficult for one firefighter to bring a Dutch rolled hose into use. In passing, it should be noted that back injuries were a major cause of lost man-days and claims for compensation in all fire services. At the very least, manually winding hoses while walking in a stooped position was likely to contribute to the problem. Normally when hoses were rolled at the fireground, the firefighter was wearing full kit. It was a very unpopular job for firefighters.

Noel had always been interested in developing new ideas and with more time on his hands after the closure of the contracting business he began to apply himself to the task of developing a product which would take the manual effort out of hose winding. In doing so, he realised that fire services were inherently conservative about adopting new products and with good reason. Operational methods were drilled into firefighters so that they would react automatically to situations. While a product that rolled hoses would not be central to firefighting it would have to be of demonstrable benefit before a service would consider purchasing it.

Noel began by developing prototypes in his workshop. When he needed specialist engineering skills he enlisted the help of his brother-in-law Terry Joyce. Terry was general manager of a plastics manufacturing company which had an engineering workshop where Noel, with the assistance of the maintenance staff at the plant, was able to further develop the product. Terry became more and more involved in the project and they eventually agreed to jointly develop the product and so set up a company, Fire Hose Technologies Ltd, in which they had equal shares.

THE PRODUCT

In the first instance, Noel set out to develop a product which would wind large diameter hoses. Over a two-year period, the product went through several major design changes and was added to with the development of a series of related products. The hose winder which finally emerged from the research bore little relationship to the original concept, though the principles remained the same.

In essence, the product consisted of a shaft, two bearings and two wheels. The bearings were fitted to a shelf in a locker on the vehicle. This was normally done under the shelf to avoid using valuable locker space. A stainless steel shaft was then inserted into the bearings. When not in use the shaft was recessed under the shelf. When required for use the locker was opened and the shaft pulled out so that it protruded about 6 inches outside the vehicle. Two cast alloy wheels of 20 inches diameter were then fitted onto the shaft and slotted in position leaving a distance between the wheels slightly wider than the width of a flat hose. The winder was now ready to receive the hose. To wind the hose, the firefighter simply lifted the coupling at the end of the hose, placed the lugs of the coupling on a fitting on each wheel, set off centre, and wound the hose by turning a handle on the outer wheel. A standard hose took 35 seconds to wind. When wound, the outer wheel was removed and the hose pulled from the shaft. The outer wheel was then replaced ready to wind the next hose. Apart from being quick and convenient to operate, the wound hose was much tighter than with manual rolling. This offered two possible advantages. Firstly, it occupied less locker space which is regarded by fire services as a valuable commodity as normally all shelf space on a vehicle is used. Secondly, it was less likely to unravel from the centre when lifted to put into use. If a hose unravelled when required it was immediately discarded until the incident was over. When all the hoses were wound, the wheels were removed from the shaft and stored on a locker wall. The shaft was again recessed under the shelf. A major factor in the technical success of the product was that the winding commenced from an off centre position thus creating a circular roll. If the winding commenced from the centre of the wheels, an ellipse would be created which would obviously not be suitable for rolling out the hose.

The winder could be fitted to either side of the vehicle though it was generally fitted to the offside near the rear of the vehicle. A patent had been registered and was eventually taken out for Ireland and the UK. The Irish fire service was closely modelled on the UK service. From what Noel and Terry understood, other fire services did not roll hoses, rather they folded them in lengths. A further factor in limiting the patent was cost. A patent covering Ireland and the UK cost under £2,000. A patent for the EU would cost £20,000 and a world wide patent up to £100,000.

THE SECOND PRODUCT

While still working on the first product Noel and Terry began to develop ideas for a further product. As previously noted, washing of hoses was also a tedious manual operation. The hose was laid out on the ground and scrubbed with a brush. It was then turned over and the other side was washed. Noel began experimenting with ways of washing the hose while it was being wound. From this research the hose washer came into being. The hose washer relied on the fact that each fire tender had a pump and a water supply. As noted already, the water supply was connected to the first aid reel hose. The hose washer, again made from stainless steel, was fitted on a bottom shelf of the vehicle beside the first aid reel hose drum. It consisted of a steel pipe about one foot in length at one end of which was a rectangular fitting. On either side of the fitting were jets which released water in a predetermined flow and angle. The washer was positioned directly under the winder when in use. The rectangular fitting also contained two brushes which cleaned surface grit from the hose prior to washing and two rubber fittings which removed excess water from the hose after washing. The other end of the washer was connected to the water supply on the vehicle by diverting it from the first aid reel hose washer. When required, a simple turn of a tap diverted the water into the washer. In addition, an inductor was fitted which introduced detergent into the washer. The power of the pump on the vehicle lifted detergent from a container at a predetermined rate and mixed it with the water. Detergent suitable for cold water usage was readily available.

To operate it, the hose winder was set up as normal, the vehicle pump was set at a pressure of between 20 and 25 bar, a tap on the washer was switched to on and the hose was fed through the washer while being wound. The jets on the washer then cleaned the hose on both sides. The angle of the jets were set to reflect the angle of the hose as it was lifted from the ground behind the tender. While the winder could function independently of the washer, the washer needed the operation of the winder to work satisfactorily.

THE THIRD PRODUCT

Noel then added a further product to the range. Using the fact that he now had a pressurised and effective supply of water and detergent he modified a lance similar to those seen in car washes and fitted 30 feet of rubber hose to it. The other end of the hose was then fitted to the outlet used by the hose washer. This enabled other items to be washed. In particular, the vehicle could be washed down effectively. It was also possible to hose down a firefighter after an incident. Noel himself had used the lance in an incident where an ebbing tide had left a deposit of oil on a slipway rendering it very dangerous. The lance, again using the pump to supply pressure, had dispersed the oil effectively. Interest had also been expressed in using the product to decontaminate men and equipment after a fire involving chemicals. The alternative to this product was a power washer which would cost up to 10 times the price of the lance washer and which could only normally be used at base as it required an electricity supply.

AND THEN THERE WERE FOUR PRODUCTS

When the first three products were demonstrated, interest was expressed in the possibility of developing a further product which could wash the two first aid reel hoses carried by a vehicle. Unlike the large hoses, the first hose was rigid and did not lie flat when not in use. It was made from rubber and had a diameter of less than 2 inches. It was used frequently and was very awkward to clean manually. Noel and Terry examined various options and developed further prototypes before eventually being satisfied with the outcome. The result was a cylinder almost one foot long and six inches in diameter. The cylinder was placed on the ground adjacent to the vehicle. A hose was fitted to the cylinder at one end and the hose washer outlet on the vehicle at the other end. A door was cut the full length of the cylinder. When this was removed, the first aid reel hose was placed into the cylinder and the door was replaced. Four jets inside the cylinder were positioned to wash the hose under significant pressure. Two guide rollers at either end of the cylinder facilitated the movement of the hose. The hose was wound onto the drum as normal except that it passed through the cylinder and was cleaned.

This completed the product range which now included:

- Hose Winder
- Hose Washer
- Power Washer

- First Aid Hose Washer.

No further additions were envisaged. Most of the fabrication was subcontracted to a local engineering company though some assembly was undertaken directly in-house. Having examined the costs involved and after discussions with interested customers, prices were set as follows:

- A complete system fitted to one side of the vehicle was £1,500.
- The winder was priced at £500.
- The winder and washer was £1,000.
- The power washer was priced at £200.
- The first aid hose washer was priced at £300.

In the case of options 4 and 5 it is assumed that the hose washer has been purchased. Otherwise extra costs could be incurred.

The products were priced to provide for a breakdown point of 60-70 complete units or £100,000 in annual turnover, though it was obviously hoped to exceed this. Noel and Terry recognised that while the price was not considered excessive by potential customers, some had commented that it was difficult to see the price in the fittings. This arose because volume for each component was likely to be low and so the cost of each component was substantial.

THE MARKET

The market was assumed to be Ireland and the UK. Fire services in both countries were in close contact and operated largely similar procedures. The products did not appear to have application in the remainder of continental Europe or the USA though this remained to be investigated thoroughly. It was estimated that there were approximately 500 water carrying fire tenders in Ireland and up to 8,000 in the UK. Each fire service in both countries was based on a local authority area such as a city or county. In Ireland there were some 30 such authorities while in the UK, where the authorities covered larger population and areas, there were some 60 authorities of which the biggest was London. Borsetshire was the second largest, serving a population of more than 2 million. The services in both countries operated independently of central control though they were subject to regular inspection and budgetary constraints. Each fire service was under the management of a chief fire officer (CFO). In Ireland, chief fire officers being newly appointed were expected to have a formal engineering qualification and were likely to have come into the position from another branch of the public service. On the other hand, all CFOs in the UK had come through the ranks of firefighters. The CFO was, in the first instance, responsible to the local authority. Each fire service had a budget for equipment, though in Ireland the allocation of resources for purchasing a new vehicle was decided at central government level.

Vehicle replacement policy depended largely on the local situation and, in particular, on usage. UK fire services appeared to have more resources than Irish services. The following replacement policy was typical. A vehicle might have a front line life of 8 years. After this period it would be relocated and used as back up or for training for a further 5 to 8 years. It was then scrapped. In passing it should be noted that the Fire Hose Technology system could be readily fitted to a new or existing vehicle.

While local fire services would be the main potential customers, there were some other users, principally airports and major industrial installations.

The system was clearly not a major purchase by fire services but it was a new product and would be likely to be assessed as such. Early orders were likely to be of a trial nature. The balance of benefits from the product between fire service and firefighter could dictate whether a service would purchase the product. Noel and Terry realised that fire services were only likely to purchase if they saw a clearly defined benefit and any repeat purchases would depend on the system being used in practice.

While services were independent, they maintained relatively close contact with each other and so product news would be likely to travel relatively quickly. There was also some evidence that some fire services were more innovative than others but it was difficult to establish this. They were not necessarily the biggest services.

Fire service management was relatively easily identified though it was much more difficult to establish clear roles on the purchase of a new product. In addition titles varied from service to service. The Borsetshire example may or may not have been typical and in any event took several visits by Noel and Terry to establish.

- Chief Fire Officer Phil Archer was in overall command of the brigade. His role appeared to be largely a policy-making role with little involvement in day-to-day operations. However, in this instance, he had been a useful first contact and had attended the first demonstration at brigade H.Q. Thereafter he had no role in the process.
- Deputy CFO Tom Forrest appeared to be responsible for operations. He appeared to have a major influence in the purchasing process for a new product, though he also remained in the background after the initial demonstration.
- Operations Officer Joe Grundy was the main contact. His principal role appeared to be responsibility for manpower. He attended all meetings and demonstrations.
- Brigade Engineer Sid Perks had nominal responsibility for all technical purchases but indicated to Noel and Terry that he would not have a significant influence in the decision process.
- Purchasing Officer Brian Aldridge appeared to only be concerned with routine purchases.
- Station Officer Paul Carter was in charge of the headquarters fire station. His official role seemed to be minimal but he appeared to Noel and Jerry to be quite influential and was well disposed towards the product.

In Ireland, as the services were smaller, management frequently rested with at most two or three senior personnel. The CFO again dealt with policy while the assistant CFO took charge of operations. However, from what Noel and Terry had seen, not much happened without the involvement at some stage of the CFO.

UK fire services appeared to mostly deal directly with manufacturers with few intermediaries involved. In Ireland, on the other hand, the market was much smaller and most items were imported. As a result, most sales tended to be through distributors, many of whom served other markets such as fire extinguishers, first aid and fire prevention equipment. The market was dominated by two or three large players, though the general equipment market for small ticket items such as fire extinguishers was very scattered and was characterised by easy entry. Noel and Terry had developed a close relationship with one of the major distributors who had been very helpful. But in view of the relatively easy access to the market Noel and Terry wondered whether it made sense to enter into a distribution arrangement.

Promotion was mostly through attendance at trade fairs. There was one major exhibition each year in the UK which also tended to attract Irish fire service management. However, apart from the cost of exhibiting, which would run to several thousand pounds, display was also a problem as a proper demonstration needed a fire tender and much open space. In Ireland the two principal annual events were the Chief Fire Officers Conference in May and the Fire Engineers conference in October, which was attended by ranks below that of CFO. Both conferences had small trade shows attached which were available at a relatively low cost. The conferences rotated around the country and were normally organised by the local fire service. Both conferences attracted a considerable number of delegates from the UK who appeared to greatly enjoy Irish hospitality.

There was one specialist monthly magazine called *Fire* which serviced the industry in the UK and was also circulated in Ireland.

With regard to vehicle manufacturing there were three major UK manufacturers and one in Ireland. These fulfilled orders to the exact specification of the fire service purchasing the vehicle.

THE COMMERCIALISATION PROCESS

The product was first brought to public attention in May of 1993 when Noel and Terry attended the CFO Conference in Bantry, Co. Cork. A prototype winder was demonstrated and attracted considerable interest in particular from UK CFOs, one of whom was the Borsetshire CFO. In all about six UK CFOs expressed interest in obtaining further information, though it was made clear to them that much work remained to be done. In general the reaction was very heartening. Noel spent the rest of 1993 refining the winder and developing the washer. It was a long, tedious process with many false starts. Early in 1994, the product was demonstrated on an edition of the popular TV chat show, "The Late Late Show". Once a year the programme was dedicated to enterprise development. A fire tender was borrowed for the day and was drawn up outside the studio with much hooting of sirens. In total the product received over a minute of airtime on a prime time show. Even after this showing, further major revisions were undertaken. By April of 1994 the first three products were ready. A few systems were sold locally but the major thrust was to start developing the UK market. Contact was renewed with the CFO of Borsetshire, a major UK midland fire service. They were targeted for their size, interest and ease of access by car ferry when transporting goods. A demonstration was organised which was attended by all senior management at brigade HQ. As a result, a complete system was fitted, excluding the first aid reel hose washer which had not been developed by then. Following discussions with Borsetshire, the system was sold for £1,000. Borsetshire preferred to purchase rather than simply have a trial as it placed them in more control and Noel was glad of the money, little as it was, because development costs were mounting. Research and development assistance had been provided by the local development agency but Noel's resources were now limited as indeed were Terry's. Terry also realised that he could only devote limited time to the project though he visited Borsetshire on three or four occasions with Noel.

The arrangement with Borsetshire was that the system would be fitted to a fire tender operating in a busy urban area. Noel fitted the system and visited Borsetshire about every two months, partly to check on progress and also for discussions with Grundy and others on the first aid reel hose washer which was, by then, being developed. The arrangement with Borsetshire was that they would log usage and comments over a trial period which could run from three to six months. At a visit after two months the brigade engineer confided to Noel and Terry that if the trial was satisfactory, the brigade would purchase between 50 and 70 full units for use in major full-time stations. Visits to the station where the system was fitted indicated that the firefighters were pleased with the system and, most importantly, were using it. However, Noel was obliged to show them, on a few occasions, how to get full use from the system and he realised that he would have to prepare a users manual.

While the trial was in process, Noel and Terry took a decision that they would not make any further contacts in the UK until the trial was complete. They felt that any other service would ask who else had purchased the product and on being told that the product was on trial in Borsetshire would await the results of the trial. However, in October of 1994, Noel again demonstrated the product at the Fire Engineers Conference in Cork. Again there was some interest among UK visitors and a few new contacts were made. The product had also been shown but not demonstrated at the equivalent conference in 1993 but attracted no interest. A demonstration seemed to be an essential marketing tool.

The trial in Borsetshire continued in fact for six months until November. Noel again spoke to Grundy who was now the main contact. Grundy arranged an appointment for Noel and Terry and, as indicated at the start of this case, gave Noel to understand that he was ready to do a deal on a multiple purchase. They had always found Grundy awkward and extremely abrasive, though he appeared to be popular and well known to firefighters in the stations which Noel and Terry visited and he had also taken a proprietorial interest in the product. For the visit in mid-December Noel and Terry had brought the final version of the first aid reel hose washer. In order to demonstrate this, they needed to use the tender on which the system had been fitted. To their surprise, the tender had been moved a few weeks previously to a quieter station. The firefighters at that station had no idea of what the system was for and had not used it. But worse was to follow. Noel and Terry knew that there had been severe and highly localised flooding in Borsetshire the previous weekend. Several lives had been lost and the fire service had been severely stretched. Grundy claimed that the service had lost up to £2 million in damaged, ruined or lost equipment. For this reason, he told Noel and Terry they would not be purchasing any of the hose systems. His parting remarks were: "I have no money to spend on toys" and "Can this be dismantled — the guys where it was have become fond of it and want it back".

His attitude appeared to have changed completely and the meeting was over in less than 30 minutes.

WHAT NEXT?

The pints of stout were working their oracle and the pair began to calm down though they were still in a state of shock. Terry, with some experience of deals that failed to materialise, had not been as confident as Noel that a deal was assured. However, it was Noel, and not Terry, who had dealt with Grundy. With a long wait to the ferry, they began to take stock. They recognised that they would have to start selling quickly or the project was doomed. Their resources were limited and Terry would not be in a position to devote any time to the business after Christmas due to his other commitments. They knew that they required promotional literature but had delayed producing this until the full product range was ready. Now this was being overtaken by limited resources. Decisions were going to have to be taken quickly on several points.

- Should they continue to seek direct sales or use an agent or distributor in the UK with consequent implications for margin and price. Noel had no selling experience.
- Either way, how could or should they promote the product?
- Might some organisation be interested in licensing the product?

They also pondered what Grundy had said, unsure as to whether he meant it. How was the product really seen by fire services? Certainly all had different priorities and different product benefits seemed to appeal to different services. One, for example, had cited a study which they had carried out on leaks in hoses. This had shown that most leaks were caused by particles such as grit adhering to the hose. Then when the hose was rolled and stored on a moving vehicle, the abrasion caused further leaks. The Fire

Hose Technology system solved this problem, yet when this was mentioned to management from another service they showed no interest at all. A reassessment of product benefits also seemed to be essential but where should they start? There were still several hours before the ferry sailed.

3

NORTHERN IRELAND TOURIST BOARD: "FACING THE FUTURE"

Maeve McArdle

INTRODUCTION

Unlike any other tourism organisation in Europe, the Northern Ireland Tourist Board (NITB) has had the unenviable task of promoting a country locked in bitter conflict as a potential tourist destination.

Over the past 25 years the Board has adapted to the difficulties associated with "the troubles". In fact the Board has now to recognise the possibilities and opportunities that continued peace means for the economy of Northern Ireland and in particular tourism.

According to Ian Henderson (CEO), the NITB is:

> "At present experiencing a surge of interest in tourism. But tourism booms and surges can be short lived. We are more interested in harnessing the world's attention currently focused on us to continue our work in establishing Northern Ireland's tourism industry so that it becomes an important part of this society with long term growth potential" (*Tourist News*, 1994).

Recent data indicates an increase of 3 per cent (in real terms) in tourism revenue from £173 million in 1993 to £183 million in 1994. Enquiries into the Dublin office increased by 78 per cent in the last twelve months and by 339 per cent comparing December 1993 to December 1994.

Market changes have shown an increase in pure holiday visitors from the Republic and Great Britain by 14 per cent and 8 per cent respectively.

The main challenge faced by the Northern Ireland Tourist Board now is to attempt to transform Northern Ireland from being a place where tourism is a nice added bonus to a place where it is a very important part of the economy.

BACKGROUND

The Northern Ireland Tourist Board was established in 1948 and was the first regional tourist board set up in the UK. Working with and funded by the Department of Economic Development (DED), the Board has responsibility for developing sustainable tourism in Northern Ireland.

In 1988, following seventeen years of civil unrest and constant fluctuations in tourism trade in the North, the government commissioned a review of tourism in Northern Ireland.

The Tourism Review Group (June 1989) made a number of recommendations to the Department and the Board. The Group believed that the most effective approach would be the creation of a Northern Ireland Tourism Development Organisation with responsibility for both marketing and product development, bringing together the promotional role of the Northern Ireland Tourist Board and the grant-aiding functions of the Department of Economic Development.

The Tourism (Northern Ireland) Order 1992 enacted on April 1st of the same year completed the restructuring of the NITB, and subsequently the Board became the single authority responsible for tourism in Northern Ireland.

Today the Board is funded by the DED and by funds through the International Fund for Ireland (IFI) and European community programmes. These funds are distributed to assist worthwhile projects in the private and public tourism sectors. The Board assisted numerous projects to the value of £2.3 million in 1993/94.

Table 1 includes the mission statement and objectives of the NITB.

TABLE 1: MISSION STATEMENT AND OBJECTIVES

NITB Mission Statement

"To develop and present Northern Ireland as a quality tourist destination within the international market, to promote domestic tourism and to maximise the tourist industry's potential as a significant creator of wealth and jobs in NI".

The Objectives of the NITB

The Boards' key objectives are as follows:

1. To promote NI as a quality competitive tourism destination.
2. To attract investment and develop the tourism product and enhance its quality.
3. To work with district councils and develop a regional approach.
4. To work in conjunction with the Training and Employment Agency, towards establishing and supporting an effective and efficient training mechanism for the tourist industry.
5. To provide and maintain professional comprehensive visitor services.
6. To stimulate and inspire the increased involvement of the public and private sectors in tourism activity.
7. To continue the development of a highly effective and efficient, results driven, organisation.
8. To undertake the research, evaluation and monitoring necessary to ensure the effectiveness of the activities of the Board and the industry.

Source: NITB Corporate Plan, 1992-1995

MARKETING IN THE NITB

From 1968-1979

In 1968 the Board appointed its first marketing manager whose role was to establish an intensive selling programme in Britain and the Republic of Ireland and initiate research into the type of tourist market on which the board should concentrate.

In the following year the marketing department developed and introduced new marketing techniques. More money was invested in advertising and promotion which lead to a national TV and newspaper advertising campaign. However, later in that same year the world became aware of Northern Ireland when "the troubles" began. The Board continued to collaborate with the British Tourist Authority (for the UK) and Bord Fáilte (for the South) in the US.

Due to the continuing civil unrest, the NITB declared Northern Ireland as "unsaleable" in 1972 and adopted a low profile approach to marketing. The Board cancelled its national advertising campaign in Britain, the Republic and elsewhere.

The conditions in NI forced the marketing department to focus on new ways to market Northern Ireland. The focus adopted was to maintain contacts with Bord Fáilte and BTA. Niche strategies were used by the Board to encourage local industries to invite their foreign counterparts to come to Northern Ireland for a holiday.

In 1975 the decision was made again not to invest in a national campaign as research indicated that this money would be wasted and the campaign might prove counter-productive.

While Britain and ROI remained effectively "off limits" the Board cultivated markets overseas focusing on those countries least sensitive to Northern Ireland politics and reports of violence. The following year the Board had some success with this strategy as the Continent had dropped Northern Ireland from its headlines and became more preoccupied with other news stories. A "hard sell" approach was adopted in Holland, Belgium, Switzerland and Germany.

Throughout the rest of the 1970s the NITB developed niche strategies, focusing on activities and special interest holidays such as golfing and coarse fishing.

The decade ended on a brighter note with increased numbers of visitors from America, Canada, Australia and Europe. The Board produced a Tour Operators Guide for the first time in eight years and new offices were opened in Europe and North America in 1979.

From 1980-1995

In the early 1980s the Board began to re-establish itself in the Republic of Ireland by concentrating on the activities market, participating in the annual Holiday and Leisure Fair in Dublin and continued collaboration with Bord Fáilte in the North American market.

The marketing department explored the possibility of expanding into new markets and so researched the potential of Australia and New Zealand. Home holidays were vigorously promoted by the "Invite a relative home" and the "Home Coming" campaigns in 1982.

This strategy of developing new markets and slowly reintroducing Northern Ireland back into the key markets was followed for a number of years. In 1987 the Board appointed a marketing manager in the Republic. By this time the Board had left behind the low profile approach and had returned to marketing the product in the Republic and Britain.

In 1988 the Board continued to focus on ROI and GB and targeting territories producing the largest number of pure holiday visitors i.e. Europe, North America and Australasia.

The "North by Nassau" and "North Bound" advertising campaigns ran in the Irish Republic in 1990 and 1991.

The current promotional campaign offering the slogan "The Northern Ireland you'll never know unless you go" started running in 1992 and is still as effective today. According to Paul Lavery (Marketing Manager) the campaign uses the most important asset of the Northern Ireland, "the friendliness and warmth of its people".

For the last number of years the Board has published a marketing opportunities handbook which outlines the strategy for the following year. The strategy for 1995 and beyond is to focus and develop the pure holiday visitors market in all the key markets.

TABLE 2: PAST AND PRESENT PROMOTIONAL MESSAGES

	Promotional Campaigns
1969	"Northern Ireland: not many people seem to know about it."
1982	"Invite a relative home" (domestic campaign).
1990/91	"North by Nassau" and "North Bound" (Republic of Ireland).
1992-present	"The Northern Ireland you'll never know unless you go."
Present	"And you thought you'd seen it all" (domestic campaign).

Source: NITB Annual Reports 1965-1993

TOURISM — THE PRESENT POSITION

In 1994 the Northern Ireland Tourist Board earned £242 million in tourism revenue (£228 million in 1993) of which £59 million came from domestic tourism. The Board estimated that 1.29 million (out of state) tourists visited NI in 1994 and that visitor tourism expenditure was £183 million.

The most significant change was seen in the holiday visitors market which increased by 10 per cent to 276,000.

FIGURE 1: STAYING VISITORS REVENUE COMPARISON 1992 AND 1993

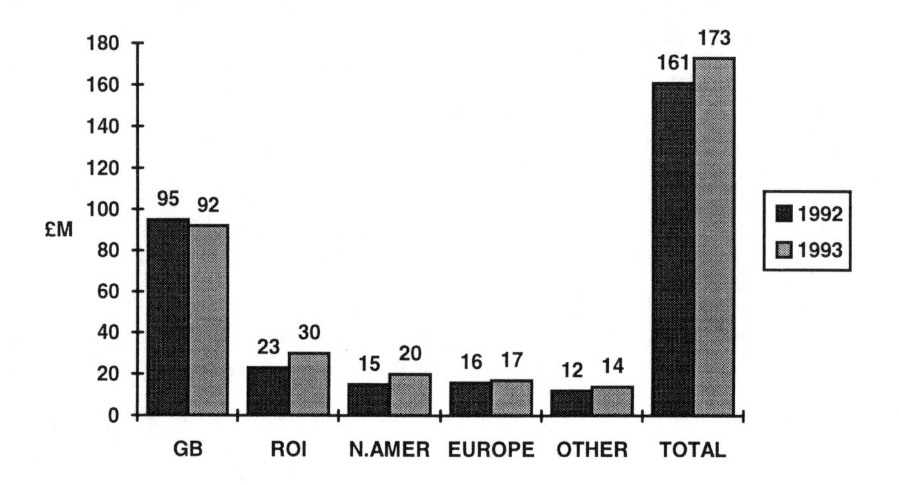

Source: NITB Annual Report, 1993.

The targets set by the NITB in the Corporate Plan have not been achieved; however, based on the world-wide recovery, estimates for 1994 and 1995 are more favourable.

The main purpose for visiting Northern Ireland in 1993 was given as Visiting Friends and Relations 41 per cent, Business 30 per cent, Holiday 20 per cent and other 9 per cent. (See Appendix D for main purpose of visiting in the past).

Today GB and ROI account for 86 per cent of the out of state market for NITB. The Republic is the largest single source of PHVs (pure holiday visitors) providing 40 per cent (125,000 in 1994). Research by the NITB has shown that almost 80 per cent of

PHVs enter through the Irish Republic crossing over the border to Northern Ireland.

These markets are considered the "bread and butter" markets of the NITB. It is because of this the Board has invested many of its resources into marketing in these countries.

KEY MARKETS — STRATEGY

Republic of Ireland

Statistics from Bord Fáilte show that domestic and overseas tourism in the Republic passed the £2 billion revenue mark in 1993 (£642 million from domestic tourism). This represented an increase in tourism revenue of 52 per cent over the past five years.

TABLE 3: PURPOSE OF VISIT (OVERSEAS)

Main Purpose of Visit to the Republic:	
Holiday	43%
Visiting Friends/Relations	25%
Business/Conference	19%
Other	12%

Source: Bord Fáilte — Tourism Facts 1993

In 1993 the Northern Ireland Tourist Board recorded a 16 per cent increase in holiday visitors to 110,000 (from 1992) while total visitor numbers from this market grew by 6 per cent to 373,000 generating a revenue of £30.1 million.

Recent research has shown that almost 72 per cent of ROI residents have never been to Northern Ireland for an over night stay. This represents a large potential market on Northern Irelands doorstep.

The Republic of Ireland presents a double opportunity for the NITB: firstly, ROI residents (who take in excess of four million home holidays each year), and secondly, the overseas visitor (3 million of whom visit the ROI annually).

TABLE 4: PURPOSE OF VISIT TO NORTHERN IRELAND (BY IRISH RESIDENTS)

Visiting Friends and Relatives	26%
Holiday	30%
Business	26%
Other	18%

Source: NITB Tourism Facts 1993

The strategy outlined by *Marketing Opportunities 1994/95* for this market is to consolidate the efforts of 1993. This will include a new promotional campaign exclusive to ROI group buyers; continued participation at regional fairs; intensified special interest promotion; co-operation with the trade; continued TV advertising and intensified press and public relations activity to increase awareness of Northern Ireland as an attractive, accessible holiday destination.

Great Britain

Revenue generated by this market dropped by almost 3 per cent in 1993 to £92.4 million (£95 million in 1992). Although revenue has dropped, this market generates almost 50 per cent of the total market.

Almost 50 per cent of visitors from this market identified the purpose of their visit was to visit friends and relations (VFR), 35 per cent for business reasons and around 19 per cent were pure holiday visitors (PHV).

The PHV market in GB can be divided into three main categories: short break holidays, special interest holidays (e.g. golfing and fishing) and the all-Ireland holidays. The strategy for 1995 is to turn the increased awareness and interest in Northern Ireland into bookings.

The strategy will involve a series of holiday exhibitions, participation in main trade events, special interest activity promotions, major advertising campaign and continued liaison with the main tour operators.

The Domestic Market

Domestic tourism earned £55 million in 1993 and £44.6 million in 1992. Domestic holiday makers took 675,000 trips in 1993, 275,000 long trips (4+ days) and 440,000 short trips (1-3 days), spending £34 million and £21 million respectively.

The Board describes its objective to position Northern Ireland as a "stand alone" destination, with an emphasis on the activity and special interest sectors. The key to the marketing strategy is to develop the off-peak season.

The NITB hopes to achieve this through advertising in brochures, press and radio promoting the theme "and you thought you'd seen it all". Also through participating in trade fairs and consumer shows as well as collaborating with local companies on joint projects.

FIGURE 2: DOMESTIC TOURISM REVENUE 1972-1993

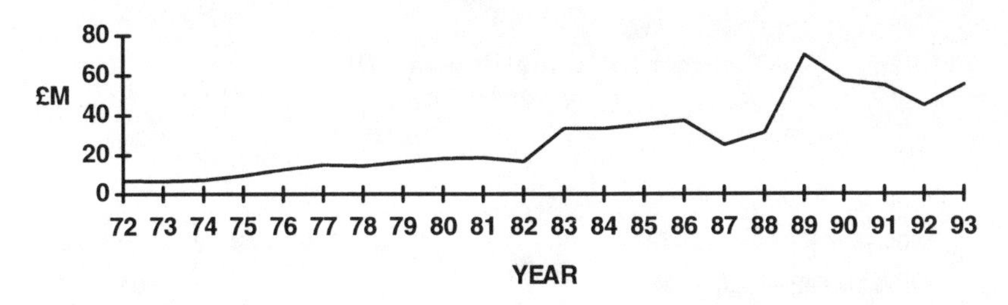

Source: NITB Annual Reports 1972-1993

WORLD TOURISM

Tourism is one of the world's most important growth industries. The World Tourism Organisation figures show that tourism arrivals rose from 25 million in 1950 to 500 million in 1993. Revenue from tourism was $324 billion, an increase of 9 per cent on 1992 and represents 5.5 per cent of world GNP.

Future trends in world tourism indicate a swing away from Mediterranean sun-type destinations towards long-haul "green" regions. This would indicate an opportunity to market Northern Ireland as an alternative destination.

THE TOURISM ECONOMY IN NORTHERN IRELAND

Northern Ireland has seen significant growth in tourism in the last five years and revenue generated by tourism in 1993 was £228 million. Tourism's contribution to GDP is put at between 1.2 and 1.3 per cent.

Employment in tourism-related activities in the North accounts for 10,000 jobs, or 1.8 per cent of the workforce, compared to 6 per cent in ROI and 8 per cent in Scotland. A recent report by the Northern Ireland Economic Research Centre (NIERC) suggests that if the level of tourism in NI reached that of Scotland or ROI that perhaps 10,000 more jobs could be created.

FIGURE 3: TOURISM REVENUE IN REPUBLIC OF IRELAND AND NORTHERN IRELAND 1984-93

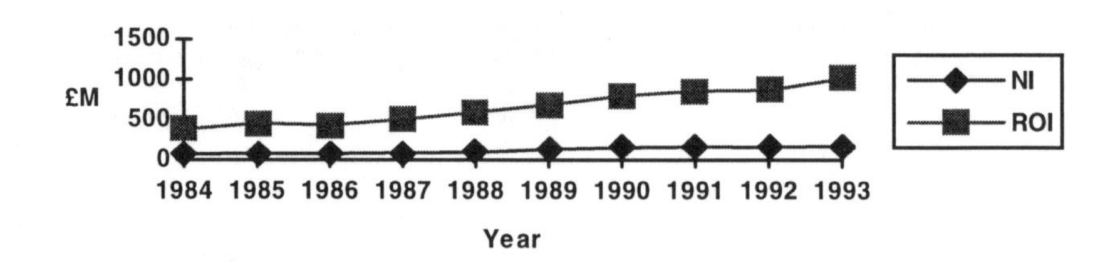

Source: NITB Annual Reports and Bord Fáilte Diary 1994

IMAGE PROBLEMS

Tourism is a fragile industry as it is a high risk investment for tourists; they want the best they can get out of their limited holiday time and money.

The Board described "image" as one of its weaknesses in its Corporate Plan. For 25 years, the NITB have tried to market a unique but somewhat troubled product to the world.

Northern Ireland has been locked in a bitter and violent constitutional dispute since the late 1960s. Every day since then the world has been given the latest news on the "war" in the North by the world media, images of violent acts are printed in newspapers and flashed across TV screens world-wide.

Due to the image factor the NITB kept a low profile in the early 1970s recognising the inappropriateness of marketing the product during the troubles. While tourism grew elsewhere the NITB saw a dramatic slump in their trade. In the late 1970s a report on the tourism industry in the UK identified NI as its weakest sector.

The image problem has been a major challenge for the Board as they struggle to capitalise on the VFR (visiting friends and relations) market and all the time building on the core product.

On the other hand the Board recognises the "curiosity factor" as one of its strengths:

> Many people around the world have heard of Northern Ireland but often for the wrong reason. The opportunity to harness this "curiosity factor" should not be overlooked as a positive factor in encouraging people to visit and understand Northern Ireland.

The Corporate Plan (1992-1995) suggests that NITB should try to take advantage of this curiosity factor.

Current promotional campaigns emphasise the attractions of NI with the slogan: "The Northern Ireland you'll never know unless you go". This strategy is used to encourage customers to see the Northern Ireland they have never seen before and to satisfy their own curiosity about the place.

Since the IRA and Unionist cease-fires, curious Southerners have made their way northwards to sample the culture and delights that the North has to offer. NITB reports that the number of enquiries in the Dublin Information Centre have increased by more than 75 per cent since last January. A recent report by Cooper and Lybrand suggest that there will be a positive economic impact resulting from peace in the six counties.

DEVELOPMENT PLAN

In May 1994, the Board published the draft document for a development strategy for the years 1994-2000. This strategy is a successor to the *Indicative Plan* published in 1989 and builds on the structures put into place following this plan. The objective is to identify the areas of opportunity for future development. The plan sets about recognising the weaknesses of the NITB and making these problem areas a priority.

A recent performance review focused on the changes in the tourism product of Northern Ireland. This review identified the need for development in many areas, including visitor attractions and accommodation.

TABLE 5: VISITOR ATTRACTIONS GROWTH RATE IN 1993

The average growth rate in visits to attraction is 4.2%	
Historical properties	+2.1%
Wildlife	-7.4%
Museums Visitor Centres	+3.1%
Workplaces	+19.6%
Country and forest parks	+7.9%
All Attractions	+4.2%

Source: Development Plan, 1994-2000

Accommodation

Bed stock in Northern Ireland currently stands at 21,832. This comprises of Hotels, 7,385; Guest houses, 2,272; B&Bs, 7,548; Self Catering, 2,540 and Youth Hostels, 2,087. Average annual room occupancy in Northern Ireland's hotels during 1993 was 48 per cent. Over the past five years it has been consistently around 50 per cent.

Figure 4 highlights the development priorities for NITB for the next five years.

FIGURE 4: DEVELOPMENT PRIORITIES FOR NITB, 1994-2000

Activity and Special Interest Tourism	**Attractions**
Priorities	*Priorities*
Walking	Natural heritage
Cycling	Cultural heritage
Riding	Industrial heritage
Golf	**Accommodation**
Angling	*Priorities*
Boating	Hotels
Canals	Guest houses
Water sports	Bed and breakfasts
Bird watching	Self catering
Conferences	Youth accommodation
Genealogy	Camping
The arts and tourism	Caravan parks

Source: NITB Tourism in NI — A Development Strategy 1994-2000, May 1994.

Economists indicate that the potential for tourism growth is good. They have estimated that the North's tourism revenues of £228 million could have been 30 per cent higher without "the troubles".

Recent joint marketing initiatives with Bord Fáilte in the US continue to build on the co-operation between the two organisations in the past. Perhaps the next logical step is to develop a single authority responsible for promoting all Ireland, both North and South.

The "backing winners" approach used in the past has proved successful for the NITB. How will the Northern Ireland Tourist Board approach the challenge presented by peace in Northern Ireland?

APPENDICES

A. DEFINITIONS

A Visitor
Any person visiting for any reason other than following an occupation remunerated from within the country — any country other than that in which he has his usual place of residence

A Tourist
Any visitor staying at least 24 hours in the country visited. Tourists as defined may be subdivided into three groups:
1. Those engaged in leisure pursuits — the holiday makers.
2. Business People.
3. Those visiting friends and relatives (VFR Traffic).

To these categories add a fourth category — the home tourist — the Northern Ireland resident holidaying away from home but in his own country.

B. MARKETING DEPARTMENT NITB 1994/95

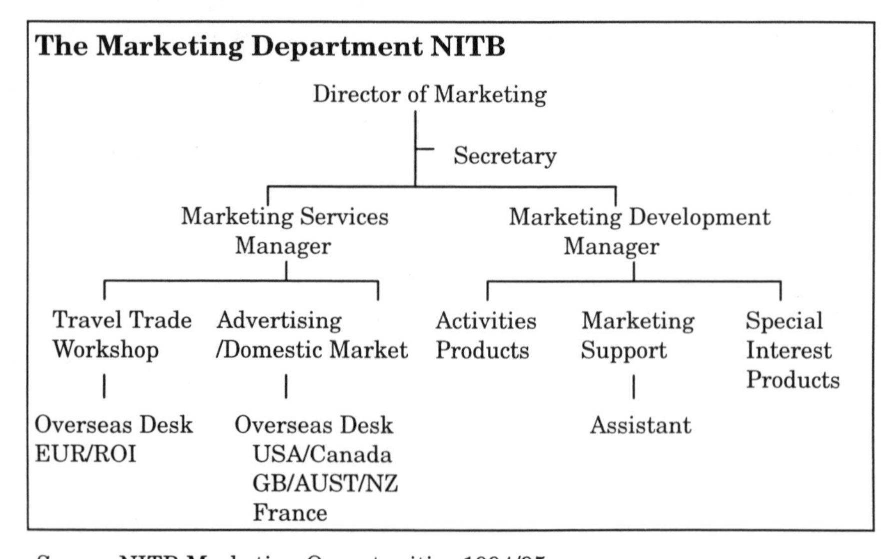

Source: NITB Marketing Opportunities 1994/95

C. Top Tourist Attractions, 1993 (in 000s)

1.	Giants Causeway Visitor Centre	370
2.	Ulster Museum	246
3.	Ulster Folk & Transport Museum	181
4.	Belfast Zoo	170
5.	Malone House & Barnett Demesne	150
6.	Dunluce Centre	135
7.	Ulster American Folk Park	131
8.	Belleek Pottery	125
9.	Waterworld	112
10.	Linen Hall Library	91
11.	Portstewart Strand	85
12.	Carrick-a-Rede Rope Bridge	68

Source: NITB Tourism Facts

D. Purpose of Visit to Northern Ireland (in 000s)

Year	*VFR*	*Holiday*	*Business*	*Shop*	*Others*
1974	179	20	78		4
1975	186	17	90		5
1976	171	9	82		6
1977	203	8	88		6
1978	357	64	163		44
1979	409	118	178		23
1980	426	99	161		24
1981	344	79	149		16
1982	424	118	145		25
1983	451	116	172	66	60
1984	455	126	191	70	66
1985	450	111	168	63	71
1986	428	106	184	48	58
1987	473	117	211	46	96
1988	456	125.4	226.8	35.3	86
1989	545	158.8	260.3	19.3	107
1990	516	222.1	294.4	20	99.5
1991	456	262.9	333.9		132.8
1992	510	247	380		117
1993	519	251.1	377.6		113.8

Source: NITB Annual Reports 1974-1993

E. TOURISM REVENUE GENERATED IN NORTHERN IRELAND

Year	*£m*	*Year*	*£m*
1965	23.0	1980	90.2
1966	24.5	1981	78.6
1967	26.5	1982	84.8
1968	28.4	1983	225.6
1969	24.5	1984	105.6
1970	22.7	1985	113.7
1971	20.0	1986	119.0
1972	36.5	1987	116.3
1973	39.4	1988	127.8
1974	47.4	1989	206.3
1975	59.5	1990	210.0
1976	67.1	1991	216.6
1977	81.5	1992	205.6
1978	99.6	1993	228.0
1979	133.2		

Source: NITB Annual Reports 1965-1993

Change of Methodology

A. 1972	Total Revenue = £
B. 1972	Method (total includes): Visitor Revenue = £ Home Holiday = £ Carrier Revenue = £
C. 1980-1983	Method (total includes): Staying Visitors = £ Day Excursionists = £ Home Holidays = £
D. 1984-present	Method (total includes): Visitor Revenue = £ Domestic Revenue = £

F. SELECTION OF CURRENT PRINT ADVERTISEMENTS, MARCH 1995

THE HEAD GARDENERS OF NORTHERN IRELAND DON'T USUALLY ENCOURAGE VISITORS TO TAKE CUTTINGS. THE COUPON IS A RARE EXCEPTION.

In our gardeners' care, you'll discover some of the finest gardens in these islands. Mount Stewart, for instance. Prized by the National Trust as one of its greatest gardens, Mount Stewart's attractions include intricate topiary, 'the Sunken Garden', based on a design by Gertrude Jekyll, and a terrace inhabited by stone dodos.

Tropical birds of a more animated sort fly overhead in a greenhouse at the National Arboretum, at Castlewellan. Not far away, there's Rowallane, celebrated for its rhododendrons and azaleas.

Equally unmissable are Belfast's spectacular Lady Dixon Park Rose Gardens and the Botanic Gardens' Palm House and Tropical Ravine. Not to mention Antrim's newly restored seventeenth century formal gardens. And the many private gardens open to visitors under the Ulster Gardens Scheme.

Of course it's a truism that garden enthusiasts are the nicest of people. So who could be more deserving of Northern Ireland's famously friendly welcome, her renowned restaurants and extremely accommodating range of places to stay? To find out more, simply treat the coupon the way generations of gardeners at Mount Stewart have treated yew and box. Clip it.

For your guide to Gardens, complete your name and address details and send to Northern Ireland Tourist Board, P.O. Box 6, Dun Laoghaire, Co. Dublin.

Mr/Mrs/Ms ____________________
First Name

____
Second Name

Address ____________________

____

____

THE NORTHERN IRELAND YOU'LL NEVER KNOW. UNLESS YOU GO.

Northern Ireland Tourist Board

F. SELECTION OF CURRENT PRINT ADVERTISEMENTS, MARCH 1995 (CONTINUED)

FINDING YOUR WAY ON FOOT IN NORTHERN IRELAND? YOU MIGHT NEED A COMPASS. YOU WILL NEED SCISSORS.

It would be folly to rush the experience of Northern Ireland's unspoilt countryside or historic towns. That's why walking pace is the recommended speed limit throughout the province.

Wherever you're based you'll find varied and dramatic scenery on your doorstep. To help you in your explorations, use the scissors to clip the coupon. We'll send you a guide detailing fourteen great walks in Northern Ireland, some planned with the adventurous hill-walker in mind, others requiring a little less effort.

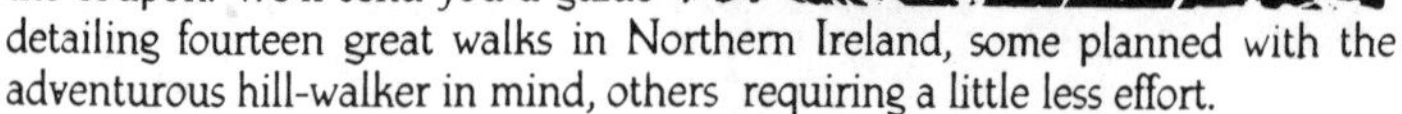

So spend a day following a cliff path on the spectacular Antrim Coast. Or devote a weekend or longer to the Mountains of Mourne. And at journey's end: a chance to sample some of our famous hospitality at the local pub, restaurant or country guesthouse. Of course, there's no rush on a walking holiday in Northern Ireland. But don't let that stop you sending off the coupon by return of post.

THE NORTHERN IRELAND YOU'LL NEVER KNOW. UNLESS YOU GO.

Northern Ireland Tourist Board

For your guide to Walking, complete your name and address details and send to Northern Ireland Tourist Board, P.O. Box 6, Dun Laoghaire Co. Dublin.

Mr/Mrs/Ms ____________ First Name

____________ Second Name

Address ____________

ST 3/95

F. SELECTION OF CURRENT PRINT ADVERTISEMENTS, MARCH 1995 (CONTINUED)

Miles of quiet, secluded rivers; a wealth of lakes, large and small – visit Northern Ireland and let yourself in on one of game angling's best kept secrets.

Wade the classic fly water of the Mourne in search of salmon. Drift Lough Erne for wild brownies. Or hook into a grilse on the Bush or Bann. Whatever your quarry, you'll soon discover that some of Europe's best fishing is located amongst beautiful and unspoilt scenery.

The one thing that's sure to be spoilt is you. With only a short distance between one river or lake and the next, variety is guaranteed and promising new waters are never far away. As for accommodation, the angler can opt for anything from the freedom of self-catering to the luxury of a country house hotel.

The region holds many other attractions for the angler; those unique species of trout the dollaghan, sonaghan and gillaroo for instance. No less unique is the friendliness of the welcome you'll receive wherever you go. So find out more. Send us your name and address today.

BEFORE WE INTRODUCE YOU TO THE SALMON AND TROUT OF NORTHERN IRELAND, WE'LL NEED TO KNOW YOUR NAME.

For your guide to Game Fishing, complete your name and address details and send to Northern Ireland Tourist Board, P.O. Box 6, Dun Laoghaire, Co. Dublin.

Mr. Mrs. Ms ______________
First Name

____
Second Name

Address ______________

____

____

____

THE NORTHERN IRELAND YOU'LL NEVER KNOW. UNLESS YOU GO.

G. HOTEL OCCUPANCY JANUARY 1995

HOTEL OCCUPANCY SURVEY
MONTHLY REPORT — JANUARY 1995

Summary of Results

Average room occupancy for January rose 10 percentage points to 46 per cent the January 1994 level. This is the highest level recorded for the month of January since records began. Average bedspace occupancy increased by 6 percentage points to a record level of 27 per cent.

Visitor content average 66 per cent, an increase of 7 per cent over the same period last year.

By Classification

All classification sectors with the exception of unclassified hotels showed increases when compared with last year's results. Four star hotels showed the best year-on-year improvement in room occupancy, increasing 31 percentage points, giving an occupancy level of 55 per cent.

Three star, 2 star and 1 star hotels increases by 6, 10 and 3 percentage points to record room occupancy levels of 48 per cent, 40 per cent and 38 per cent respectively. Unclassified hotels fell by 4 percentage points to record an occupancy level of 37 per cent.

By Region

All areas of the Province with the exception of the South West showed increases when compared with January 1994. The Belfast region showed the highest increase with a rise of 18 percentage points to give occupancy levels of 53 per cent, 37 per cent and 40 per cent respectively. The South West region fell by 6 percentage points.

Sample size was 70 Hotels with 2322 bedrooms.

G. HOTEL OCCUPANCY (CONTINUED)

OCCUPANCY SURVEY BY CLASSIFICATION AND BY REGION JANUARY 1995

			Average Room Occupancy (%)						Average Bedspace Occupancy (%)						Visitor Content* (%)					
Classif-ication	No. of Hotels	No. of Bedrooms	Monthly		Weekend		Weekday		Monthly		Weekend		Weekday		Monthly		Weekend		Weekday	
			'94	'93	'94	'93	'94	'93	'94	'93	'94	'93	'94	'93	'94	'93	'94	'93	'94	'93
****	4	365	55	24	43	19	63	28	37	14	34	14	40	15	87	83	77	68	92	96
***	25	1111	48	42	40	34	53	49	26	23	26	23	26	23	60	57	48	42	68	69
**	18	419	40	30	33	27	45	33	25	18	26	21	25	16	59	38	43	22	70	53
*	17	282	38	35	28	29	46	40	24	21	20	20	27	22	64	65	49	57	73	72
Other	6	145	37	41	29	39	43	41	23	25	21	29	24	22	79	74	72	61	84	84
Average			46	36	37	30	52	41	27	21	26	21	27	20	66	59	53	44	75	71
Region																				
Belfast	15	897	55	37	40	27	65	45	35	21	29	18	40	23	91	85	84	73	94	93
N West	8	265	53	38	39	27	64	46	29	21	24	18	33	25	71	65	67	64	73	66
N East	20	453	37	33	35	31	38	35	22	20	26	25	18	17	43	37	30	22	54	54
S West	11	240	29	35	29	33	28	37	17	22	21	27	14	18	36	28	27	18	44	38
S East	16	467	40	36	35	34	44	39	22	19	24	22	21	17	51	51	39	40	58	62
Average			46	36	37	30	52	41	27	21	26	21	27	20	66	59	53	44	75	71

* "Visitors to Northern Ireland" as a percentage of total arrivals.

G. Hotel Occupancy (continued)

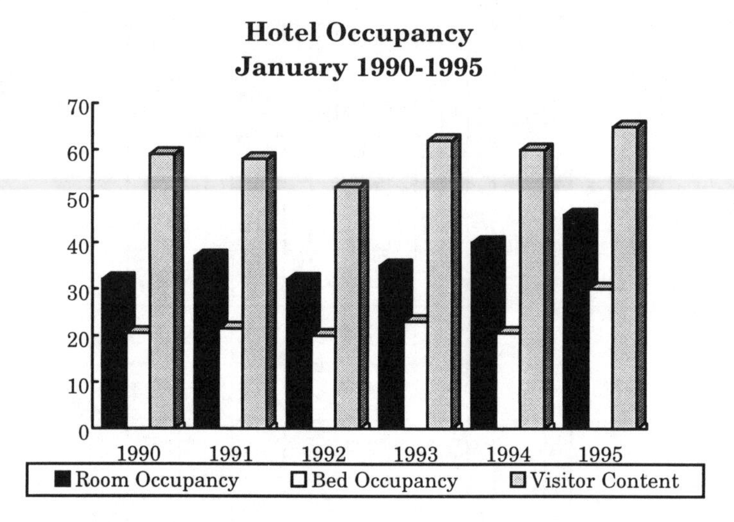

Source: NITB Research Department

H. Total Enquires January 1995

	January '95	*January '94*	*% Change*
Belfast	16,597	8,489	+95.5%
British Travel Centre	391	307	+ 27.4%
Dublin	5,649	1,836	+ 207.7%
Frankfurt	1,078+	628	+ 71.7%
Glasgow	875	—	—
London	1,998*	1,691	+ 18.2%
New York	1,942	2,479	- 21.7%
Paris	184	211	- 12.8%
Toronto	539	554	- 2.7%
	29,253	16,195	+ 80.6%

* Includes 566 responses re Ad Campaigns. + Includes 89 Swiss Enquires

I. VISITOR TOURISM TO NORTHERN IRELAND 1994

Summary Statistics

			% change on 1993
a	Total visitors to Northern Ireland 1994	1,294,000	+3%
b	Total holiday visitors 1994	276,000	+10%
c	Total revenue from visitor tourism 1994	£183m	+3% (real terms)

Market Area Analysis

	Total Visits (000s)	% change on '93	Holiday Visits (000s)	% change on '93
Great Britain	708	(+1)	66	(+8)
England and Wales	538	(+3)	41	(+17)
Scotland	170	(-)	25	(+4)
Republic of Ireland	390	(+5)	125	(+14)
Europe	87	(+6)	44	(+2)
Germany	28	(-3)	19	(+6)
France	14	(-)	7	(-22)
Holland	8	(+14)	2	(-)
Italy	9	(+13)	5	(-17)
Other Europe	28	(+17)	11	(+22)
North America	77	(+10)	29	(+7)
USA	54	(+17)	22	(+16)
Canada	23	(-4)	7	(-)
Australia/NZ	20	(+11)	9	(-)
Elsewhere	12	(-20)	3	(+50)
Total	1,294	(+3)	276	(+10)

Source: NITB Research Department

Bibliography

Business & Finance (1994): "Northern Ireland Open For Business", 8 December 1994.

Coopers & Lybrand (1995): "The Peace Dividend", IMPACT, European Publication, January: 37-47.

Department of Economic Development (1988): "A view to the Future", Tourism Review Group.

Griffith, J.R. (1984): "Northern Ireland — Putting the Record Straight", *Tourism Management*, 5: 138-144

Goodall, B. and Ashworth, G. (1988): Marketing in the Tourism Industry, Kent: Croom Helm.

HMSO (1992): The Tourism (Northern Ireland) Order 1992.

Irish Times, "NI Tourist Numbers Grow by Only 1%", 27 August 1994.

Management (1994): "Peace Dividend or Peace Deficit", December 1994.

NITB (1994): "Tourism in Northern Ireland — A Development Strategy 1994-2000", Consultative Draft Document, May 1994.

NITB, Marketing Opportunities 1994/95

NITB, "Survey of Visitors Attractions (1993) Report", Research Department March 1994.

NITB, "Survey of Hotel Occupancy" 1993 Research Department, April 1994.

NITB, "Annual Report 1993", 46.

NITB, "Corporate Plan 1992-1995".

NITB "Local Authority Tourism Estimates 1989-1993", Research Department 1993/94.

Phelps, A. (1986): "Holiday Destination Image", *Tourism Management*, 168-180.

Richter, L. and Waugh, W. (1986): "Terrorism and Tourism as Logical Companions", *Tourism Management*, 7: 230-238.

Smyth R. (1986): "Public Policy for Tourism in Northern Ireland", *Tourism Management*, 120-126.

Sunday Business Post, "North Elite Bites Golden Bullet", 11 September 1994.

Sunday Tribune, "Business Ready for the Peace Dividend", September 1994.

Ulster Business, "NITB Outlines a Record Year", September 1994.

White, D. and McGee, J. (1995): "Tourism Going for Growth", *Business & Finance*, 23 March 1995: 18-19.

Wilson, D. (1993): "Tourism Public Policy and the Image of Northern Ireland Since the Troubles", in O'Connor and Cronin, *Tourism in Ireland — A Critical Analysis*, University College Cork.

4

NORTH CLARE LEADER TOURISM PROMOTIONS: A CASE STUDY IN RURAL TOURISM MARKETING

Alex Gibson

INTRODUCTION

The management committee of North Clare LEADER Tourism Promotions was holding its first meeting of 1995. As the meeting drew to a close, and members prepared to leave the warmth of Lisdoonvarna Enterprise Centre to brave the January cold, they were cheered by the news that the organisation's application to join the national umbrella marketing organisation for rural tourism — Irish Country Holidays — had been successful. Sheila Quinn, the organisation's full time marketing executive was particularly pleased, feeling that this was a development that would add greatly to the area's marketing effectiveness. Certainly, when reviewing the marketing activities of the first two years of the organisation's operations, a record of continuing progress and sustained increases in visitor numbers was evident.

However, several major marketing issues remained unresolved. Among such issues the crucial one of how to limit the phenomenon of "corridor tourism" loomed large. The fact that the majority of tourist flows through the North Clare area were of a transitory nature had long been acknowledged by the organisation's management committee. Tourists en route from the higher profile tourism sectors of Kerry and Galway tended to pass through the area, generally taking in only the main, non-paying, attractions of the Cliffs of Moher and the Burren.

There was a clear need to encourage tourists to stay longer and increase their average spend in the area. Specifically, the organisation had targeted the "rural tourism" customer as a likely source of sustainable revenue in the future. These visitors generally stayed several days in an area seeking the authentic countryside experience. However, in seeking to attract such visitors, it was clear that several key, and apparently generic, issues centred around the marketing of rural tourism, would have to be addressed:

- The problem of marketing products that were largely uncontrollable by the marketer.
- The essentially intangible and indefinable nature of the product.
- The fragmented, variable, and increasingly fragile, nature of the product base being marketed.
- The reliance on the activities of the national tourism organisation to influence national and regional tourism numbers and flows.
- The costs involved for essentially voluntary organisations in effectively marketing overseas.
- The need to strike a balance between the desire to energise the community effort in supporting marketing initiatives, and the need for decisive action on marketing decisions.

BACKGROUND

North Clare LEADER Tourism Promotions Ltd. began operations, as a community founded limited co-operative, at the beginning of 1993, based in offices in the Enterprise Centre in Lisdoonvarna. The initial funding of £101,000 to be spent over two years was secured from the LEADER co-ordinating company for Clare County, Rural Resources Development Ltd. (RRD). (For a more detailed discussion on the LEADER funding structures see Exhibit 1.) This funding level was matched by the local community, either in the form of contributions by local tourism providers or through voluntary donation of time and expertise. This particular matching process was an important feature of the LEADER scheme and demonstrated a clear emphasis on the principle of "bottom up" approaches to management that was a core element of the scheme.

An initial committee of 24 was drawn from representatives from twelve major villages in the North Clare area. Initially, two full time staff were employed; a marketing executive, Sheila Quinn, and a personal assistant, Sue Targett. Office space was rented in the Enterprise Centre, Lisdoonvarna. A management committee of five was drawn from locals who voluntarily gave their services, while the salaries of the marketing executive and assistant were paid by FÁS, the State training agency. FÁS also paid the salaries of part-time staff employed in the five Tourism Information Points opened by North Clare LEADER Tourism in its first year of operation. Accordingly, the total allocation of £101,000 made by RRD to North Clare LEADER Tourism was to be spent solely on marketing activities and associated administration costs over the period 1993/1994.

One of the characteristics of rural tourism marketing was the complex nature of the organisational structure required. Unlike private organisations, the administration of rural tourism involved a complex web of inter-organisational linkages with a backdrop of involvement from several Government departments (Exhibit 2).

The marketing assistance to the North Clare community was one among many such initiatives nationally to promote increased levels of, and professionalism in, marketing activity at community level. A rush by local areas to develop a coherent and well marketed tourism product was evident with over 30 distinct local tourism co-operatives existing nationally, most under the umbrella organisation Irish Country Holidays. In addition, over 200 applications for grant assistance under the Operational Programme for Rural Development 1994-99 were awaiting assistance in the Agri-Tourism Grant Scheme totalling £16 million. It was evident that North Clare LEADER Tourism would have to develop a long-term marketing strategy to develop a sustainable competitive advantage given the high degree of projected fragmentation in the rural tourism sector.

CONCEPT OF RURAL TOURISM

Attempts to define the concept of rural tourism had been varied and lacking in core themes. However, rural tourism could be generally viewed as a concept which covered tourist activity devised, managed, and marketed by local people, and based on the strengths of the natural and human environment.

While it was agreed that rural tourism encompassed many activities, this definition offered a distinction between rural tourism and agri-tourism (which was focused solely on farm activity and land), and between rural tourism and green tourism (green tourism being focused on a general ethos of being environmentally-friendly which could be equally applicable in cities). This definition, then, distinguished rural tourism from tourism activity in coastal resorts, cities, and winter sports resorts. It also clearly recognised the dynamic role of the community in the fostering of rural tourism projects.

GROWTH OF RURAL TOURISM IN IRELAND

The concept of rural tourism was not new. Indeed, it had long enjoyed recognition as a sector of tourist activity; however, its development and promotion on a more significant scale in Ireland had been much more recent. Initially the growth of rural tourism arose as a direct result of the accommodation supply shortages in the 1960s when farmhouses took in guests, encouraged by both Bord Fáilte and their own organisation, Fáilte Tuaithe.

The more recent emphasis on the development of rural tourism as a viable tourism strategy could be part attributed to the economic situation in rural Ireland. The continual reduction in Common Agricultural Policy price supports to farmers, and the imposition of quota controls, had necessitated alternative uses of rural land. However, this was not the sole driving force behind the growth in rural tourism.

Rural tourism was growing in popularity due to demand rather than supply factors. The rural tourism consumer had a high degree of interest in culture, heritage and health issues; specifically, they had a high degree of environmental awareness. Whilst defining the market was difficult it was probably best done by exclusion. It was not the coach tour market nor the transient, touring individual. Rather, it was a person or groups who were seeking an environmentally friendly experience in an authentic setting.

TOURISM IN IRELAND

The tourism sector continued to enjoy rapid growth in Ireland, as in most of the developed world. The sector's share of GNP had increased to 7 per cent in 1993, from its 1988 level of 5.8 per cent. The increased status of tourism as an engine for economic growth was finally being realised in a concrete way with a high degree of Government, private and EU investment, valued at £652 million, being planned over the course of the Operational Programme for Tourism 1994-1999. The Programme's direction broadly followed the strategic direction outlined in the "Tourism Task Force" Report of 1992, and set a target of £2,250 million in annual foreign exchange earnings by 1999, and targeting an increase in employment of 35,000 (full-time equivalents).

The Programme also heralded an increased emphasis on the marketing of the tourism sector, with a sum of £125 million being allocated over the six year period for marketing activities, apportioned as follows:

ERDF	£51 million
National Public	£5 million
Private Sector	£69 million

A key objective of the plan was the integration of the public and private components, with four key strategic objectives governing the operation of the plan. Any tourism enterprise or organisation would need an appreciation of the need for the "dovetailing" of their activities with those of the macro policy makers. The key marketing objectives set in the Operational Plan were:

- Extending of the tourist season — e.g. support for annual festivals outside the season.
- Expansion of sea and air access route — support for carriers promoting Ireland.
- Development of new markets, e.g. Spain, Switzerland, and Scandinavia.
- Development of product and niche markets such as equestrian, and language learning.

- Attraction of more high-yield business such as incentive, shopping excursions and car-hire traffic.

TOURISM IN THE SHANNON REGION

County Clare was part of the natural and administrative area known as the Shannon Region, where the primary State agency responsible for the tourism sector at the regional level was Shannon Free Airport Development Company Ltd. (SFADCo). The other areas under the SFADCo umbrella were Counties Limerick, Tipperary North Riding, North Kerry and South Offaly. SFADCo were primarily responsible for the tourism promotion of the region as a whole. SFADCo had been highly successful in such activities, with overseas visitors' expenditures in 1992 up over 20 per cent versus 1988 (Exhibit 3).

SFADCo priorities which had a particular bearing on the marketing of North Clare were to develop new products with the emphasis on matching products to identified market niches such as rural tourism.

SFADCo identified the "Atlantic Rim" coastline of West Clare and North Kerry as possessing a variety of scenic areas and coastal resorts. Indeed its identification of major tourist flows reflected the reality of a "tourism corridor" being in existence in County Clare. The organisation's most recent report on strategic planning of tourism in the region had included an audit of accommodation resources on an area by area basis (Exhibits 4-6). SFADCo identified rural development in general as being of strategic importance to the success of the administrative area, planning a total spend on rural development, including rural tourism, of £12 million over the period 1994-99. The overall objective for SFADCo over the 1994-99 period was to achieve annual revenue increases of 10 per cent, up from the 6 per cent growth rates being achieved in the period 1988-92. This was expected to prove difficult given the Government's decision to modify the Shannon Stopover Policy.

RURAL TOURISM: THE EUROPEAN CONTEXT

Tourism in the countryside had a long history in Europe. Much of the rise of rural tourism in Europe was linked to the great wave of urbanisation which took place, leading up to and following the Second World War. In this period, vast population shifts took place away from rural areas to the industrialised cities. Indeed, a substantial proportion of the early rural tourism clientele was composed of these new city dwellers returning to their "own" countryside to visit those they had left behind there. Visitors were often accommodated by friends and family. Where a rural tourism sector existed as such, standards of comfort and the provision of comfort tended to be modest.

By the 1980s, the move away from mass tourism in Europe was well established. In addition, the rise of individualism, changes in preferences for the type of holiday setting, growing interest in sports, health and sightseeing, the search for authentic small-scale destinations all contributed to growing popularity for the rural tourism experience. These changes in attitudes were paralleled by changes in patterns of holiday-taking by Europeans, leading to shorter holidays being taken more often during the year and the development of the short-break market. The profile of holiday taking for main and short break holidays is illustrated in Tables 1 and 2.

TABLE 1: TYPES OF HOLIDAY DESTINATION (MAIN HOLIDAY)

	Countryside	*Mountains*	*Cities*	*Seaside*
	%	%	%	%
Belgium	25	19	5	55
Denmark	35	14	40	42
Spain	27	19	27	53
France	29	27	18	51
Greece	8	11	20	70
Ireland	27	8	37	46
Italy	11	24	19	58
Luxembourg	19	29	17	62
Netherlands	39	32	21	36
Portugal	29	8	24	62
Germany	34	30	15	44
UK	29	13	19	58
EU Average	25	23	19	52

Source: "Europeans and Their Holidays", Commission of the European Communities, in Davidson, R., *Tourism in Europe*, Pitman, London, 1992.

TABLE 2: TYPES OF HOLIDAY DESTINATION (SECOND HOLIDAYS) FOR COUNTRIES WHERE AT LEAST 20 PER CENT OF THE TOTAL POPULATION TAKES MORE THAN ONE HOLIDAY.

	Countryside	*Mountains*	*Cities*	*Seaside*
	%	%	%	%
France	29	33	22	28
Netherlands	49	26	24	19
Denmark	34	13	36	27
Britain	38	8	25	36
Italy	13	33	21	37
Germany	30	29	33	15

Source: "Europeans and Their Holidays", Commission of the European Communities, in Davidson, R. *Tourism in Europe*, Pitman, London, 1992.

Changes in attitudes and holiday taking patterns were accompanied by changes affecting the quality of the holidays sought by those choosing rural tourism. These demands were for high levels of comfort, service and above all, a supply of activities to keep the holidaymakers entertained and active during their stay. Consequently, there was a rise in the number of farm tours, cycling and walking tours, cultural activities, craft courses, health-related activities and a wide range of water and land-based activity sports helping to attract customers into the European countryside. This rise in activity pursuits was also clearly reflected in the Irish visitor statistics shown in Exhibits 7 to 9. In 1993, Bord Fáilte, in a specific report on rural tourism found that approximately 10 per cent of all holidays taken in Europe were based in the countryside. The report identified the following as major target markets for rural tourism in Ireland: Germany, France, Netherlands, Switzerland, Austria and Scandinavia (Exhibit 10).

In addition to the changes in the attitudes of the holidaymaker, there were also significant changes in the attitude of the commercial sector towards rural tourism.

Tour operators were increasingly reappraising their attitudes towards this sector, and more and more rural tourism products were finding their way into tour operators' brochures. Finally, as well as seeing changes in the attitudes of the holidaymaker and tour operator, tourism was also being regarded differently by those living in the countryside. The demand for rural tourism products was met by a corresponding move on the part of local communities to respond; in many instances this was prompted by declining agricultural prospects and strong initiatives at European Union level to stimulate activity on rural tourism activities.

NORTH CLARE: PRODUCT PROFILE

North Clare LEADER Tourism had the task of marketing the tourism services available in the North Clare region, covering 12 villages and their hinterlands: Ballyvaughan, Corofin, New Quay and Carron, Doolin, Ennistymon, Fanore, Inagh, Kilfenora, Lahinch, Liscannor, Lisdoonvarna and Miltown Malbay.

However, the areas with the most international recognition were two natural landscape features: the Cliffs of Moher and the Burren. The Cliffs of Moher extended for about 5 miles to the north of Liscannor and were among the highest in the British Isles with a sheer fall of 700 feet. The popularity of the Cliffs could be gauged from the fact that they attracted 55,000 visitors to the Cliffs of Moher Centre in 1992 making it the sixth most popular tourist attraction in the Shannon Region (Exhibit 11).

The Burren area attracted an estimated half million visitors annually. It was a unique area of 100 square miles of limestone terrain dating from the Ice Age situated in the centre of the North Clare region. Glacial erratics dotted the slopes and terraces and the surface water percolated to lower depths through tunnels and caves often reappearing as turloughs, flooding fields and valleys. A wide variety of plants and flora provided a rich environment for exotic species of butterflies and moths. This rich tapestry of unique flora proved a magnet for visiting botanists and painters from around the world. The Burren also contained a rich heritage of remains from ancient civilisations including Poulnabrone Dolmen and Poulawack Cairn.

The Burren Display Centre in Kilfenora, which was the gateway to the Burren, was a highly attractive interpretative centre attracting over 45,000 visitors annually. At the edge of the Burren, the Ailwee Caves, the second most popular paying tourist attraction in the Shannon region, attracted 80,000 visitors annually. The Caves contained an appealing series of stalactites, stalagmites and a waterfall.

DEVELOPMENT OF VISITOR ATTRACTIONS

In addition to the natural heritage of the region, a huge variety of initiatives had been undertaken to develop appealing visitor attractions in the twelve villages of the North Clare region. A sample of the wide variety of activities and attractions available is detailed in Exhibit 12. Notable activities available for the visitor included a visit to the Spa town of Lisdoonvarna, where one could have a mineral bath or imbibe the pungent waters of the iron, magnesia and sulphur springs. At Lahinch, the golfer had a choice of two golf courses, including the 102-year-old Championship links; in addition, the village had a 2-kilometre-long beach and a whole range of facilities appropriate for a family seaside holiday.

North Clare was also renowned world-wide as the home of traditional Irish music, with the villages of Doolin and Miltown Malbay, where the annual Willie Clancy Music School is held, acting as a mecca for legions of devotees throughout Europe and beyond. The village of Doolin was also a major embarkation point for the Aran Islands, a popular day trip option for visitors to North Clare.

Corofin was an ideal base for lake fishing in the North Clare lakelands centred in Corofin, Tubber and Ruan. The Clare Heritage centre located in the village offered a genealogical service to the growing numbers of people researching their Clare ancestry. North Clare was an ideal natural base for activity and special interest holidays such as walking and cycling. A walking and cycling brochure had been published which had helped heighten the profile of North Clare for activity based holidays. These brochures had been distributed as part of a targeted mail shot to cycling and walking clubs in 1993. A comprehensive Walking Guide detailing over thirty suggested walking itineraries was produced in 1994. An example of the Burren Way Walk, taken from the guide, is included in Exhibit 13. A recent audit of the accommodation base had also been conducted by North Clare LEADER Tourism (Exhibit 14). It concluded that there was a wide variety of different types of accommodation available, with the greatest expansion in recent years having taken place in the self-catering sector, where several group cottage schemes had sprung up along the coast.

CONSTRAINTS ON MARKETING

The management committee had identified that major constraints on the development of these products included signposting and access. North Clare LEADER Tourism recognised the need to co-ordinate and package these products in a more professional way. For the visitor attracted to fishing, a brochure was published offering helpful information. However, there has been a major decline in the angling market due to pollution and budgetary constraints for the maintenance of its lakes. North Clare LEADER Tourism was actively involved in meetings with the local communities, LEADER and Shannon Regional Fisheries Board to endeavour to deal with this problem. A consultant had been appointed to do a biological survey on its lakes to determine what is involved to bring them back to their original position on the angling market.

The Board of North Clare LEADER Tourism was acutely aware of the need for tourism product development to take place in a sustainable way. Indeed, the concept of sustainability in tourism was dominant in planning discussions. Sustainable tourism saw conventional tourism as an eternal triangle of forces, with host communities, visitors and tourism businesses in an unstable relationship, often leading to a degradation in areas and ultimate destruction of the resource base. Sustainable tourism concepts meant that the marketing of an area had to take place within a clearly defined social context. It was felt that the long term building of loyalty to an area would be dependent on such areas been demonstrably concerned for long term protection of the environment.

Further, more specific product development issues that were identified by the management committee included the following (what was often noted by those directly involved in the tourism industry was how little direct influence they exerted over most of the factors identified):

- Legal access for tourists pursuing activity holidays and visiting some major attractions
- Underdeveloped lakes for angling purposes
- No all weather leisure facilities

- Insufficient Bord Fáilte approved accommodation in certain areas
- Walking and cycling treks currently unsigned
- Poor roads and parking facilities
- Poor water supply
- Lack of adequate sewerage systems
- Insufficient public toilets
- No product branding
- Insufficient training/education courses.

POSITIONING STRATEGY

In positioning itself, North Clare LEADER Tourism paid particular attention to marketing the destination as a traditional rural one. The expectation of the tourist seeking a rural holiday was to experience a country holiday, based in an environmentally excellent rural area with access to special interest and activity holidays such as walking, cycling, horse riding, turf cutting, thatching, cheese making, etc. This approach appeared to meet with a strong degree of local approval; in the 1994 Product Provider Survey the vast majority of respondents agreed with the overall marketing decision to position Clare as a traditional area, with an emphasis on special interest holidays. The positioning decision was one that required a great deal of consideration of alternatives. The potential for pooling the resources of the various LEADER tourism promotion groups throughout the county was obvious. However, it was clear that reservations existed at local community level about such a move. Concern was expressed about the level of control that might realistically be exerted from communities over a "county-wide" budget. Moreover, the execution of such a strategy was uncertain. A recent study by management consultants had positively evaluated the "county-wide" potential, but had recommended further research into specific branding approaches that might be employed.

PROMOTION OF THE NORTH CLARE AREA

A central part of North Clare's tourism marketing had been the use of the brochure. Brochures were widely consulted by both trade and customers in the decision to take a holiday. Indeed, for those people without direct or indirect experience (through friends etc.) it was the only tangible representation of an essentially intangible offering. During the course of 1993 North Clare LEADER Tourism produced five colour brochures:

- General
- Walking
- Cycling
- Angling
- Diving.

In addition, two new 30 page, full colour, A5 accommodation guides were printed during 1993. One featured self-catering and camping facilities in the area, the second featured farmhouses, town and country homes, guesthouses, hotels and hostels.

The committee also produced an information sheet on traditions in the region such as turf cutting, thatching, cheese making, basket making and musical instrument making. The cost of producing such a quantity of promotional materials was extremely high at over £30,000 during 1993 alone (Exhibit 15).

Promotional literature was also targeted at the trade — tour operators, travel agents and handling agents, mainly in Ireland, the UK, Holland, Germany and France. Other countries targeted were Belgium, Switzerland, and the Scandinavian countries. Mailshots were also targeted at activity clubs. The tourist industry had been critical of the lack of information available in the past and welcomed the brochures which were produced. In addition to brochures, a range of packages was negotiated with local providers, offering the tour operator a "one stop" service for a particular activity holiday. A sample of a walking package is included in Exhibit 16. It was envisaged that there would be an increasing role for North Clare LEADER Tourism in developing such packages.

DIRECT MARKETING

It was recognised that there was a key need to look at the effective use of database marketing techniques to improve marketing efficiency for small marketing operators. A major direct mailing campaign had been conducted in 1993, targeting over 10,000 tour operators and activity clubs across Europe, using specially purchased mailing lists. As a marketing professional, Sheila Quinn foresaw an increased use of databases in tourism marketing but was frustrated by what she perceived as problems in monitoring their success. No system was in place which would identify the incremental business resulting from such activity. Moreover, often enquiries and bookings were made direct to the featured providers, thereby making an accurate assessment of the success of direct mail activity especially difficult. It was questioned how a more effective monitoring system might be introduced.

CONSUMER AND TRADE FAIRS

Personal selling to the travel trade and potential holiday makers was an integral part of the marketing mix for tourism organisations, taking up a large proportion of marketing expenditures. The small scale of many of the rural tourism organisations and their distance from source markets meant that there was a high degree of reliance on "push strategies", whereby tour operators featured areas in their brochures and took on the task of marketing the area. Quinn was conscious of the limitations of this approach, most notably the potential of a growing dependency on a small and powerful number of operators who had a large number of competing areas featured in their brochures.

Whilst attending fairs could be a costly business (Exhibit 17), Sheila Quinn was persuaded as to their ability to:

1. Increase the profile of North Clare as an ideal destination for activity and rural based holidays
2. Create awareness among the trade of the variety of accommodation and services available
3. Attract new operators into the area and build up contacts.

During the period 1993/94 representation had been made at the following trade and consumer shows:

- Holiday and Leisure Fair, RDS, Dublin — Trade and Consumer Show
- OP PAD Activity Fair, Holland
- Belfast Angling Show
- BIT International Trade Show, Italy
- Holiday Ireland Fair, Dublin
- Bord Fáilte Workshop, Galway, UK Tour Operators
- Bord Fáilte Workshop, Dublin, UK, US and Canadian Trade
- Bord Fáilte Workshop, Cork, Northern European Travel Trade
- Bord Fáilte Workshop, Galway, European Travel Trade
- European Educational Regional Partnership — European Dimension Conference, Hertfordshire
- Mitcar Trade Fair, Paris
- I.T.O.A. Incoming Tour Operators Association, Galway.

As a result of attendance at the shows and the contacts established, several visiting operators from Ireland, Germany, Holland and Austria featured the region in various tour operators' brochures for the 1994 season.

SITE VISITS

In addition to attendance at overseas fairs, personal selling of the area "on site" was a vital marketing activity. Sheila Quinn spent much of her time preparing for, and accompanying, visiting groups of tour operators around the region. Among the tour operators who visited the region during 1993/94 were:

- Erin Encounter — Ireland
- Shannon Cycle Tours — Ireland
- Reise Laden — Austria

- Footpath Holidays — UK
- English Wanderer — UK
- Paddington Tours — Holland
- Rent-a-Bike
- Thema Tours — Holland
- Agence Breize Amor — Germany
- Travel Choice — Ireland
- Arke Reisen — Holland
- Jolanthe Snijders — Holland
- Saga Holidays — UK
- Irish Welcome Tours — Ireland
- De Jong — Holland
- Amblinn — France
- Allience du Monde — France
- Free Wheelin' — Ireland
- Judith Clarke Reiser — Germany

The area also received visits from European Journalists and UK Universities (Plymouth, Aberdeen and Cornwall).

INTERNAL MARKETING

At an early stage, the crucial importance of the people dimension in the marketing of the rural tourism product was recognised. The tourist experience was highly dependent on the quality of interaction with product providers, as well as from the interaction within the broader community. It was clear that an initial marketing drive was required among the local tourism providers to build awareness and support for the task of marketing the area. Among the key activities that were arranged during 1993 to facilitate such support were:

- The holding of a meeting for public representatives of North Clare and local media to inform them of the plans North Clare LEADER Tourism had to promote tourism in North Clare and highlight the problems connected with occupiers' liability.
- Organisation of a meeting with Bord Fáilte and Clare County Council to outline the criteria for the accommodation sector becoming Bord Fáilte approved. This meeting was attended by 150 people.
- A series of consultations with Shannon Regional Fisheries Board, LEADER, and the local communities involved in the Angling product. An angling development plan was drawn up by consultants, under the aegis of the Regional Fisheries Board and local angling groups.
- A series of courses were organised in order to increase the professionalism of the personnel involved in provision of the tourism product. Separate LEADER training funds were accessed to finance the following courses:
    - ◊ Rural Community Tourism Course
    - ◊ Computer Course
    - ◊ Language Course.

In total the Tourist Information Points (TIPs) handled over 40,000 visitors annually and were viewed as an important factor in influencing the visitor to stay longer in the area. The management committee felt therefore that the staff manning the TIPs were the vital "front line" contact point between the area and visitors. All TIP staff, whose salaries were paid by FÁS, were accordingly sent on Customer Care training courses during 1994.

PRICING

North Clare LEADER Tourism had a very limited ability to influence pricing policies of individual tourism providers, where pricing policies of individual providers were governed by local and regional competitive forces. Where Tourism Information Points made reservations for tours or accommodation, a 10 per cent commission was charged to the provider.

Limited attempts had been made, in developing activity packages, to "bundle" prices so that the customer was only presented with one overall price for a series of activities. It was felt that this form of "price bundling" would increasingly become a integral part of pricing strategies for rural tourism marketing.

CO-OPERATIVE MARKETING AND BRANDING

The Tourism Task Force Report of 1992 set out a broad framework for the development of Irish tourism into the next millennium. Its recommendations were largely incorporated in the Operational Plan for Tourism in 1994. Of particular relevance to marketers of the rural tourism product was the emphasis given to the need for more co-operative marketing activities at community, and national, level. Indeed, at the rural tourism level such marketing co-operation had been a feature since the early 1990s. "Irish Country Holidays" was the marketing brand name of the National Rural Tourism Co-operative which was founded in 1990.

The idea of a such a national promotion and marketing structure was originally conceived by the following organisations:

- Irish Farmers Association
- Teagasc
- Bord Fáilte
- Macra na Feirme.

Initially, there was a total of thirteen member areas stretching from Innishowen in Donegal to Ballyhoura in Cork/Limerick. At the beginning of 1995 another three Rural Tourism Co-operatives had joined including North Clare LEADER Tourism, who joined under the "Burren Country Holiday" banner. The use of the Burren as a "mental hook" for positioning purposes appeared to have met with wide approval, even from those areas which were not technically part of the Burren. It was felt that the Burren was unique, internationally recognised and appealing to the rural tourism consumer's needs.

The national and international marketing activities of Irish Country Holidays were co-ordinated by a Marketing Executive, based in Dublin, and a National Co-ordinator, based at the Teagasc centre in Loughrea. An annual membership fee was collected from each of the local co-operatives with a commission (5 per cent) taken on reservations. By 1994, Irish Country Holidays could claim to be responsible for over 10,000 bednight bookings across the 13 member groups (Exhibit 18). Support for Irish Country Holidays was also available from Teagasc and Bord Fáilte for marketing and co-ordinating functions.

Of particular interest to North Clare LEADER Tourism was the key objective of "Irish Country Holidays", to establish strong links between Ireland and other European countries developing similar rural tourism products. It was felt that there was enormous potential for the creation of strong alliances with similar rural tourism groups throughout Europe, with technological developments greatly facilitating this objective. Already, reservations could be made at any one or combination of Irish Country Holidays member groups using the Gulliver Central Reservation system developed by Bord Fáilte. Rural tourism providers in Ireland were considered to be among the pioneers of such systems. There was also much emphasis on the development of an information/reservation system through co-operation with Inter-Regional Agri-Tourism Multi Media systems.

The advantages of membership to North Clare LEADER Tourism were thought to be umbrella marketing, representation of local co-operatives at Government departments and agencies, membership of the European Federation for Rural Tourism and establishing contacts with tourism groups throughout Europe to assist the further development of the rural tourism product. Details of the key features of an Irish Country Holidays are included in Exhibit 19.

It was recognised that Irish Country Holidays had an important role in communicating a consistent message of quality to prospective holidaymakers. The accreditation process had been stringent and several key criteria had to be met before membership was secured. A detailed list of the product specifications of an Irish Country Holiday is included in Exhibit 20.

The Board of North Clare LEADER Tourism also saw strong opportunities for further networking and co-operative marketing activities through the AEIDL, the LEADER co-ordinating body based in Brussels. It was envisaged that the AEIDL network would increasingly be a valuable source of learning opportunities about rural tourism marketing through such initiatives as Europe-wide audits on product and marketing resources and activities.

MARKETING COUNTY CLARE AS A WHOLE

The possibility of co-operative marketing among the operators in Clare had been mooted in several areas more recently. The incentive to market the county as a whole was drawn into sharp focus as the total amount of funding for the four LEADER Tourism promotion agencies totalled more than £250,000 under LEADER 1 (Exhibit 21). However, each community was concerned about the possible lack of individual identity and focus that might result were the county to be marketed as one. The North Clare area contained internationally famous landmarks which many argued were the main, if not sole, attraction for a large number of visitors. There were, however, compelling reasons for such a merger. Many felt that in the area of international marketing there was little impact possible for individual communities and that there would be a greater return for a pooling of resources on the international stage. The example of Bord Fáilte promoting the entire country rather than regions was cited as proof of the need for a more consolidated approach to marketing. However, with the approach of the decisions on LEADER 2 allocations in Spring 1995, there was still little evidence that there would be such a consolidated marketing effort.

TOURISM RESEARCH IN NORTH CLARE

A self-completion questionnaire (Exhibit 22) was drafted to enable a profile to be built up of visitors to North Clare. These questionnaires were available at the five Tourist Information Points which were opened and operated by North Clare LEADER Tourism staff; two TIPs at Corofin and Ennistymon operated independently.

The "top line" visitor statistics compiled from the 6,453 completed questionnaires in 1993 are outlined below.

TABLE 4: VISITOR STATISTICS 1993

Location	*Enquiries*	*Bednights*
Ballyvaughan	10,796	272
Kilfenora	8,678	36
Lahinch	7,109	426
Lisdoonvarna	11,773	349
Miltown Malbay	7,370	109
Corofin*	NIL	NIL
Ennistymon*	NIL	NIL
Totals	45,726	1,192

* Operated independently.

The Tourist Information Points handled enquiries from 45,726 visitors. Questionnaires were filled out by 6,453 of the visitors. Detailed statistics, on where people came from, what activities were pursued, and where they stayed, provided information to assist in future marketing. There were many favourable remarks made with regard to the helpfulness of the locals in the region. Tourist Information Points were much appreciated as a source of information. The negative comments were aimed at services such as banking, lack of sign posting, lack of public toilets, litter and amenities for children.

TABLE 5: VISITOR STATISTICS 1994

Location	*Enquiries*	*Bednights*
Miltown Malbay	7,941	301
Lahinch	9,315	334
Doolin	4,943	255
Fanore	402	0
Ballyvaughan	8,354	299
Corofin	9,155	14
Kilfenora	12,527	88
Lisdoonvarna	5,687	25
Totals	58,324	1,316

TOURISM RESEARCH — 1994 VISITOR SURVEY

The 1994 survey was conducted on the same basis as the previous year. However, more resources were available enabling a slightly more comprehensive profiling of visitors to be made. 5995 visitors completed the survey, representing some 10 per cent of visitors to the Tourism Information Points from May to November 1994 — Miltown-Malbay, Lahinch, Doolin, Fanore, Ballyvaughan, Corofin, Kilfenora and Lisdoonvarna.

TABLE 6: NATIONALITY OF VISITORS

Country of Origin	*% of Total*
Rep. of Ireland	22.5
United States	20.0
Great Britain	17.0
Germany	9.5
France	6
Australia	4.5
Holland	4.5
Northern Ireland	3
Italy	2

The primary objective of the survey, according to the North Clare promoters, was to quantify the awareness, attitudes to and usage of activity pursuits and facilities in the North Clare region and, as a secondary objective, to provide a more detailed profile of the accommodation users, informational requirements and satisfaction levels.

TABLE 7: SOURCES OF INFORMATION ABOUT NORTH CLARE

Friends/Family	51.5%
Brochure	22.0%
Travel Agent	10.0%
Tourist Board	4.0%

TABLE 8: ACTIVITY PURSUITS IN NORTH CLARE

Walking	60.0%
Visit Burren	58.0%
Cycling	23.0%
Bird Watching	8.5%
Fishing	7.0%

TABLE 9: ACCOMMODATION USED BY VISITORS

Guesthouse	22.5%
Camping/Caravan/Self Cater.	12.0%
Hotel	11.0%
Hostel	10.0%
Town and Country Home	8.0%
Farmhouse	3.5%

The survey indicated that the majority of the visitors had favourable impressions with regard to the services and facilities available in North Clare. The TIPs were appreciated and visitors frequently commented on their usefulness and praised the hospitality and service of the staff.

Unfavourable comments centred on the following areas:

- Poor sign posting
- Poor quality roads which are hazardous to cyclists
- Lack of transport
- Environmentally unsympathetic housing development
- Lack of rubbish bins
- Lack of entertainment, in particular traditional nights
- Lack of banking facilities.

There was a general recognition that the research process for North Clare LEADER required more attention in 1995.

Specifically, it was suggested that the questionnaire was becoming merely a self-selecting instrument for the recording of tourist behaviour. Even in respect of behaviour, there was a clear lack of understanding of the dynamics of tourist flows. Several studies had explored the phenomenon of "corridor tourism", where flows of visitors from Galway to Kerry were deemed to be the backbone of the tourism in Clare. Indeed, a recent SFADCo report reflected this, when highlighting main tourist routes in the Shannon Region. The North Clare research to date was inadequate at identifying the dynamics of such flows.

Additionally, there was uncertainty as to how the research might be made more continuous in nature, including the assessment and periodic tracking of attitudes and images of tourists. It was also felt that from the current research base some tentative comparisons with the national picture might prove useful.

RESEARCH AMONG PRODUCT PROVIDERS

In addition to the survey into the attitudes and behaviour patterns of the tourists, the Management Committee were anxious to assess and monitor the opinions of participating members in the marketing initiative. Accordingly a short questionnaire was sent to over 200 product providers who subscribed to North Clare LEADER Promotions. However, only 22 providers responded to the questionnaire which is shown in Exhibit 23. The key findings are detailed below, with a complete set of results available in Exhibit 24.

Despite the relatively low response rate, there was a high degree of support indicated for the overall thrust of marketing direction to position Clare as a traditional area with an emphasis on special interest holidays, with 88.5 per cent agreeing that this was the correct approach.

Key findings from the research indicated that there was a higher degree of satisfaction among respondents with overseas marketing efforts rather than domestic (80 per cent vs. 46 per cent). The Tourism Information Points that had been provided were widely welcomed, with 92 per cent feeling that they were successful. More people (42 per cent) felt that the TIPs were not financially viable than those who did (23 per cent). Only 21 per cent of respondents felt that it was possible to provide a viable monitoring system to assess incremental bednights generated by North Clare LEADER Tourism. Almost six out of every ten respondents felt that the use of an administrative office for North Clare had been beneficial.

A key finding from this research was that some 81 per cent of respondents felt that they had received good value for their money. Opinions were divided on the sensitive issue of whether to market the Clare area as one, rather than the division of effort that currently exists. Some 46 per cent felt that the county should be marketed as one whilst 50 per cent were opposed to this. There was overwhelming support for the education and training initiatives, with 84.5 per cent feeling that they were a positive development.

PLANNING FOR NORTH CLARE LEADER TOURISM

At the end of the second year of the operations of the North Clare LEADER Tourism, several planning priorities had been identified to:

- Endeavour to overcome some of the constraints listed above
- Improve on the quality of exiting tourism products
- Bring brochures up to a more professional standard
- Obtain membership of "Irish Country Holidays"
- Improve cycling and walking product with regard to signposting and packaging, and to introduce theme cycling and walking trails
- Develop Agri-Tourism, both for the casual and technical visitor
- Increase representation at trade shows at home and abroad
- Restore the quality of the Angling product
- Reduce the problem of seasonality by developing special interest packages
- Feature in as many European brochures as possible for the 1995 season
- Have more evening entertainment (traditional music etc.) for tourists
- Improve Tourist Information Points and provide visitors with professionally trained staff
- Increase bednights by 5,000, i.e. booked direct and through TIPs
- Co-ordinate marketing activities with Mid, East, and West Clare
- Provide professional marketing services including ongoing market research, market planning and a service for the travel industry

- Increase marketing activities in the area of special interest packages for both casual and academic visitors.

CONCLUSION

As the Management Committee and Sheila Quinn sought to design a strategy to achieve the 1995 objectives, four dominant concerns had emerged:

1. How might a co-ordinated approach to the development of the product at community, county and national level be effected?
2. How might the pending membership of "Irish Country Holidays" be fully exploited to the advantage of the North Clare area?
3. How might a more focused and action-oriented research process be implemented, at both community, product provider, and customer level?
4. How might the marketing budget be allocated in a more focused and efficient way?

As Sheila Quinn pondered these questions, she recalled conversations with marketing executives in private enterprises. They had repeatedly commented on how the decision making process seemed much easier in the private sector, than when it was done in a community context. Whether this was true or not, she was in no doubt as to the real distinction between the two marketing contexts.

EXHIBITS

EXHIBIT 1: THE LEADER INITIATIVE

As part of a concerted EU initiative to foster greater community led rural development, the LEADER (Liaisons entre actions de developpement de l'economie rurale) Initiative was published by the EU Commission on 19 March 1991. Following the publication of details, local groups were invited by the Irish Intermediary Body (the Department of Agriculture, Food and Forestry) to prepare and submit integrated Business Plans for their areas. The scheme in Ireland was launched in Athlone and Charleville in January 1992. The LEADER 1 scheme was for two and a half years and was valued at £20,803 million funding from the EU exchequer and £13,896 million from the Irish exchequer. With private funding expected to match that from public sources, the total value of the initiative was anticipated to be some £70 million. In LEADER 1, 17 LEADER groups were established in Ireland covering 61 per cent of the land area and 30 per cent of the population.

Rural Resource Development Ltd.

Among the successful applicants for national LEADER funds was Rural Resource Development (RRD) based in Shannon, County Clare. Of the seventeen successful LEADER applicant groups their allocation of EU funds was second highest, at £2.9 million. The RRD area's population was estimated to be 90,918, which, in common with the majority of LEADER areas, had declined — down 0.5 per cent between 1986 and 1991.

The £2.9 million funding received by RRD was allocated across project categories as follows:

Technical Support	1%
Vocational Training	3%
Rural Tourism	37%
Small Enterprise	33%
Natural Resources	14%
Other	12%

The 37 per cent allocation to Rural Tourism projects by RRD was of a diverse and geographically spread nature. Among the successful applicants for funding was a community founded limited co-operative formed by communities in the North Clare area dedicated solely to the marketing of this specific area.

Rural Resource Development Ltd. was the administrator and funder, bringing together the expertise of Rural Resource Organisation, Teagasc, Golden Vale, Clare Marts and community groups. Other important linkages included Clare County Council, Shannon Free Airport Development Company (SFADCo) and the County Enterprise Board.

EXHIBIT 2: IMPORTANT ORGANISATION INVOLVED IN RURAL TOURISM IN IRELAND

Department of Tourism and Trade
- Bord Fáilte
- SFADCo
- Regional Tourism Organisations
- CERT

Department of Enterprise and Employmeynt
- FÁS

Department of the Envrionment
- Office of Public Works

Department of Agriculture and Food
- Teagasc

EXHIBIT 3: SHANNON REGION: OVERSEAS VISITOR EXPENDITURE (£ MILLION)

Origins	*1988*	*1992*	*1988/1992*
Britian	35	44	+9
N. America	28	23	-5
Europe/Other	23	39	+16
Total	86	106	+20

Source: Tourism Strategy in the Shannon Region 1994-99, SFADCo, 1995.

EXHIBIT 4: SHANNON REGION APPROVED ACCOMMODATION STOCK

Sector	*1990*	*1992*	*1992/1990*
Hotels	84	86	+ 2
Guesthouses	400	509	+ 109
Self-Catering	165	207	+ 42
TOTAL	649	802	+ 153

Source: Tourism Strategy in the Shannon Region 1994-99, SFADCo, 1993.

EXHIBIT 5: NUMBER OF BEDROOMS BY SECTOR

Sector	*1990*	*1992*	*1990/1992*
Hotels	3057	3278	+221
Guesthouses	1807	2201	394
Self-Catering	572	1150	587
TOTAL	5436	6629	1193

Source: Tourism Strategy in the Shannon Region 1994-99, SFADCo, 1995.

EXHIBIT 6: NUMBER OF BEDROOMS BY AREA

Area	*1990*	*1992*	*1990/1992*
Clare	2510	3186	+ 676
Limerick	386	557	+ 171
Limerick City	1018	1085	+ 67
Tipperary (NR)	290	350	+ 60
North Kerry	1149	1310	+ 161
South Offaly	83	141	+ 58

Note: "Guesthouses" includes Guesthouses, Countryhomes, Farmhouses and Town Houses.

Source: Tourism Strategy in the Shannon Region 1994-99, SFADCo, 1995.

EXHIBIT 7: NUMBERS OF OVERSEAS HOLIDAYMAKERS (IN 000S) ENGAGING IN:

	1989	*1990*	*1991*	*1992*	*1993*	*93 v 89*
Angling	120	180	178	172	180	+50%
Cycling	100	103	141	164	167	+67%
Equest.	42	41	53	70	61	+45%
Golf	95	101	122	133	162	+71%
Hiking/ Hill Walking	244	n.a	247	264	323	+32%
Sailing	31	n.a	36	34	35	+13%
Cultural/Historical Sites	n.a	n.a	819	840	791	n.a
Gardens	368	372	329	294	312	-15%
Genealogy	39	n.a	53	58	58	+49%
Horse Racing	35	n.a	42	37	47	+34%
Islands	n.a	n.a	91	109	114	n.a
Religious	71	n.a	54	61	41	-42%
Theatres	n.a	n.a	107	106	84	n.a

Source: Perspectives on Irish Tourism — Activities, Bord Fáilte, 1994.

EXHIBIT 8: KEY VISITOR STATISTICS OF IRELAND (IN 000S)

	1988	*1993*	*1994 Prelim*	*1995 Target*
Britain	1,508	1,783	1,680	2,155
Continental Europe	408	945	988	1,068
Germany	113	265	274	n.a
France	111	242	233	n.a
Italy	21	116	118	n.a
Other Europe	163	322	363	n.a
North America	419	422	520	559
Rest of World	90	124	156	167
Total Overseas	2,425	3,274	3,632	3,949
Northern Ireland	582	540	n.a	n.a
Total Out-of-State	3,007	3,814	n.a	n.a

Source: Preliminary Tourism Statistics, Bord Fáilte 1995.

EXHIBIT 9: OVERSEAS TOURISTS TO THE REGIONS: PRELIMINARY 1994 ESTIMATES

	Numbers (000s)	*Revenue (£m)*	*% Change Nos.*	*% Change Rev.*
			1994 v 1993	1994 v 1993
Dublin	1,748	342.9	18	18
South East	765	111.6	16	35
South West	1,058	199.7	1	-2
Mid-West	803	114.7	4	-2
West	908	159.6	11	6
North West	456	86.5	1	15
Midlands-East	608	116.2	11	25

Note: The Mid-West region includes County Clare. No statistics are available on a county basis.

Source: Preliminary Tourism Statistics, Bord Fáilte 1995.

EXHIBIT 10: MARKETS WITH GREATEST POTENTIAL BASED ON HOLIDAY-TAKING HABITS 1990/91

	Population (million)	*No. of Outbound Long-holiday Trips (millions)*	*Countryside-based Holidays (000s)*
Germany	79	32	2000
France	57	11	960
Netherlands	15	8	900
Switzerland	8	5	920
Austria	7	2	380
Nordic Countries	21	10	300 (e)
Italy	58	8	70

Source: Product Marketing Profile, Rural Tourism, Bord Fáilte, 1995.

EXHIBIT 11: TOP VISITOR ATTRACTIONS IN SHANNON REGION

Attraction	*1992 Visitors**
Bunrattry Castle & Folk Park **	325,000
Ailwee Cave	80,000
Crag Cave	70,000
Geraldine Experience — Tralee	70,000
Craggaunowen	67,000
Cliffs of Moher Centre	55,000
Blennerville Windmill	52,000
King John's Castle	50,000
Burren Display Centre	45,000
Knappogue Castle **	41,000
Dunguaire Castle **	31,000
Birr Castle	28,000
Foynes Aviation Museum	12,000
Clare Heritage Centre	10,000
Memory Lane — Kerry	9,000
Lough Gur Centre	6,500
Damer House (Roscrea)	6,000
Nenagh Heritage Centre	5,000

* Estimated in some cases.

** Banquets included.

Source: Tourism Strategy in the Shannon Region 1994-99: A Discussion Paper, Shannon Development, 1995.

EXHIBIT 12: MAJOR VISITOR ATTRACTIONS IN NORTH CLARE

Place	*Type*	*Place*	*Type*
Ailwee	Caves	Kilfenora — Music School	Festival
Aran Islands	Islands	Kilfenora — October Festival	Festival
Ballinalackan Castle	Castle	Kilfenora — Set Dancing Weekend	Festival
Ballyallaban Ringfort	Ringfort	Kilfenora Cathedral	Ecclesiastical Site
Ballykinvarga Ringfort	Ringfort	Kilfenora High Crosses	Ecclesiastical Site
Ballyporty Castle	Castle	Killilagh Church and Graveyard	Church
Ballyvaughan	Village	Killimer/Tarbert Ferry	Shannon Ferry
Ballyvaughan Castle	Castle	Kilmacreehy Church	Church
Barbeque World Championship	Festival	Kilmurry Ibrickane Church	Church
Bishop's Quarter	Village	Kilmurry Ibrickane Graveyard	Graveyard
Burren Centre	Interpretative Centre	Kilnaboy Church	Church
Caherconnel Ringfort	Ringfort	Lahinch	Town
Cahermore (Great Stone Fort)	Ringfort	Lemenegh Castle	Castle
Cois na hAbhna	Cultural Centre	Lickeen Lake	Lake
Corcomroe Abbey	Abbey	Liscannor	Village
Corkscrew Hill	Hill	Liscannor Castle	Castle
Corofin	Village	Lisdoonvarna	Town
Corofin Genealogy Centre	Genealogy Centre	Matchmaking Festival	Festival
Corofin Heritage Centre	Museum	Merriman Summer School	Festival
Darling Girl from Clare	Festival	Micho Russell Weekend	Festival
Doolin	Village	Miltown Malbay	Town
Doonagore Castle	Castle	Miltown Malbay Railway Station	Historic Site
Doonmacfelim Castle	Castle	Moher	Cliffs

Place	*Type*	*Place*	*Type*
Doonmacfelim Wells	Holy Wells	Mount Callan	Mountain
Dough Castle	Castle	Music — A Summary of Events	Traditional Music
Dunguaire Castle	Castle	Mutton Island	Island
Dysert O'Dea	Castle	Newtown Castle	Castle
Dysert O'Dea Archaeology Centre	Museum/ Archaelogy Trail	Noughaval	Monastic Settlement
Ennistymon	Town	Noughaval Market Stone	Historical Site
Ennistymon Traditional Festival	Festival	Percy French Seminar	Festival
Fanore	Village	Poulawack Cairn	Burial Mound
Faunarooska Castle	Castle	Poulnabrone	Portal Dolmen
Festivals — A Summary of Events (1-2)	Music and Cultural	Quilty	Village
Festivals — A Summary of Events (2-2)	Music and Cultural	Rineen Monument	Historic Site
Fleadh Cheoil an Chlair (Co. Clare)	Festival	Slieve Elva	Mountain
Fleadh Nua (Ennis)	Festival	Spanish Point	Village
Gleninsheen Wedge Tomb	Wedge Tomb	St Brigid's Well	Holy Well
Gregan's Castle	Castle	St Joseph's Church (Miltown Malbay)	Church
Inagh	Village	St Laichtin's Well (Kilfarboy)	Holy Well
Kilfarboy Church	Church	Tobar Mo Ghua	Holy Well
Kilfarboy Graveyard	Graveyard	Toomullin Church	Church
Kilfenora	Village	Tullagh Ringfort	Ringfort

EXHIBIT 13: EXTRACT FROM WALKING GUIDE

THE BURREN WAY

DISTANCE: 26 miles / 42 km.

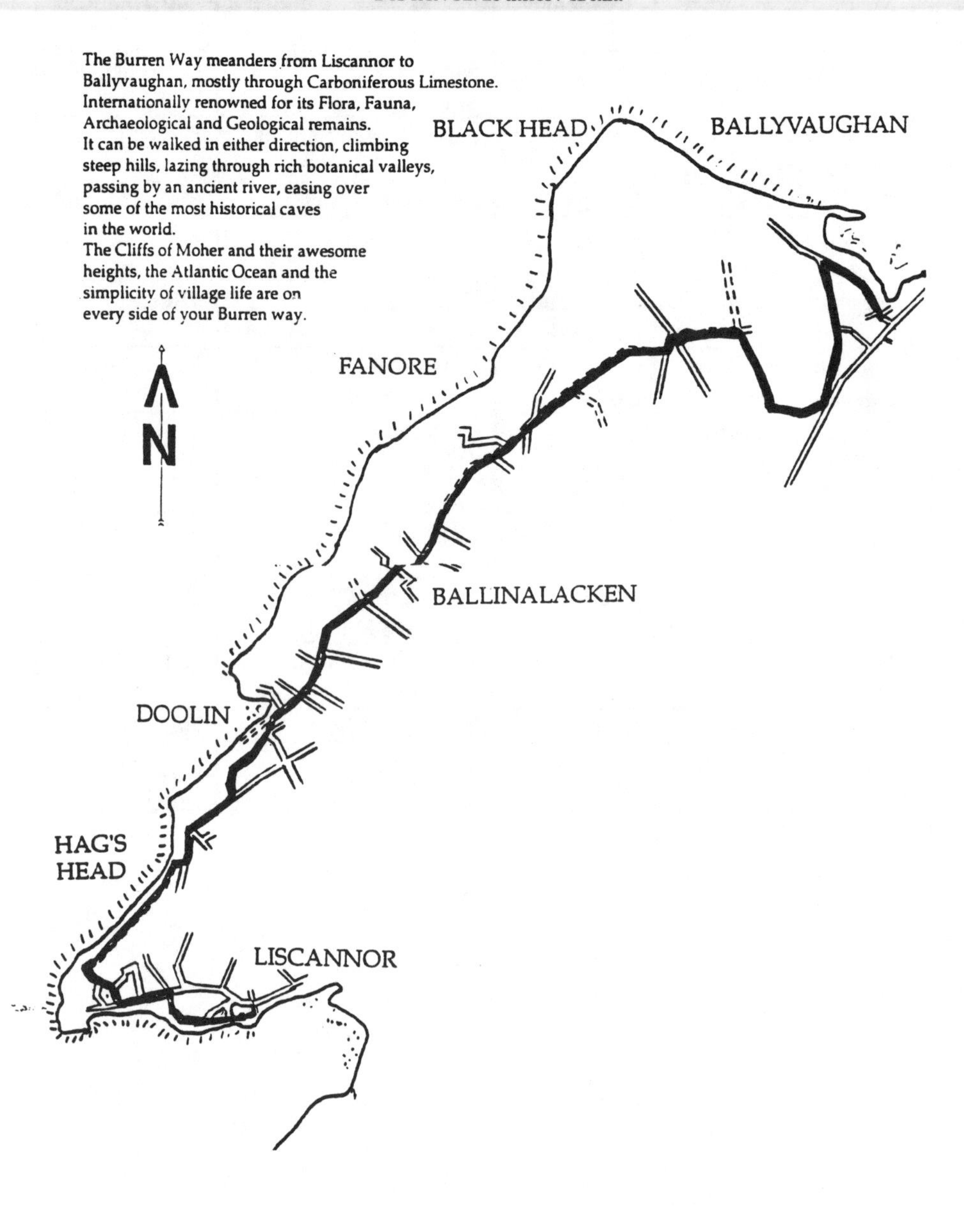

EXHIBIT 14: ACCOMMODATION STOCK IN NORTH CLARE

Accommodation Profile for North Clare LEADER Tourism* at January 1995

Farmhouses:
22 Farmhouses: 87 bedrooms: 52 en suite.

Hostels:
6 Hostels: Corofin, Doolin (2), Lahinch, Liscannor and Lisdoonvarna: 16 Dormitories, 41 rooms with average capacity of 6 persons per room.

Hotels:
12 hotels: Ballyvaughan (Grade A), Doolin (Grade B*), Ennistymon (Grade B*), Lahinch 2 (both Grade B), Lisdoonvarna 6 hotels (4 B* and 1 C), Miltown Malbay (Grade C)

Guesthouses:
Ballyvaughan — 13 Guesthouses
Corofin — 4 Guesthouses
Doolin — 16 Guesthouses
Ennistymon — 7 Guesthouses
Kilfenora — 3 Guesthouses
Lahinch — 11 Guesthouses
Liscannor — 5 Guesthouses
Lisdoonvarna — 16 Guesthouses
Miltown Malbay — 5 Guesthouses

Self Catering:
Ballyvaughan — 40 cottages, 12 bungalows
Corofin/Doolin — 11 cottages, 3 bungalows
Ennistymon — 3 bungalows, 5 cottages, 3 houses
Kilfenora — 4 cottages, 2 houses
Lahinch/Liscannor — 17 houses, 24 bungalows, 1 cottage
Quilty — 18 cottages

* Note: this list includes only those accommodation providers who were subscribers to North Clare Tourism Promotions. A small number of accommodation providers are not included therefore — largely unregistered, seasonal guesthouses.

EXHIBIT 15: BREAKDOWN OF MARKETING EXPENDITURE 1993

Activity	*£ Cost*	*% of Total*
Brochure Design, Production/Printing	30,709	65.0
Stands at Fairs	1,187	2.5
Press Advertising	721	1.5
Direct Mail Activity	13,041	27.5
Travel to Overseas Fairs	1,712	3.5
Total	47,370	100.0

Source: North Clare LEADER Tourism Promotions, Annual Report, 1993.

EXHIBIT 16: SAMPLE WALKING PACKAGE

Int. Tel. 353-65-74580.
Int. Tel. 353-65-74603.
Int. Fax 353-65-74581.

WALKING HOLIDAYS IN NORTH CLARE

7 DAY PACKAGE IN NORTH CLARE INCORPORATING CIRCULAR AND NON-CIRCULAR WALKS AND ALSO DROP-OFF AND PICK-UP ARRANGEMENTS FROM ACCOMMODATION BASE WHEN REQUIRED.

GUIDELINE PRICE FOR 1994:

IR£110.00 BED & BREAKFAST. (BASED ON GUESTHOUSE, FARMHOUSE, TOWN & COUNTRY.)

IR£65.00 BED & BREAKFAST. (BASED ON HOSTEL ACCOMMODATION.)

PRICE INCLUDES:
*ACCOMMODATION AS DESCRIBED ABOVE.
*DROP-OFF AND PICK-UP FACILITY.
*MAPS.
*ROUTE DESCRIPTION.
*PRE-BOOKED ACCOMMODATION.

SUPPLEMENTS:

SINGLE ROOM SUPPLEMENT..............IR£35.00 PER PERSON PER WEEK.

ENSUITE FACILITIES..................IR£12.00 PER PERSON PER WEEK.

GUIDE (BASED ON 6 PAX)..............IR£35.00 PER PERSON PER WEEK.

* PLEASE DEDUCT 15% FOR NETT RATE.

EXHIBIT 17: TYPICAL COSTS OF OVERSEAS FAIRS

Event	*Location*	*Content*	*Costs*	*Date*
Ferienmesse	Vienna	Consumer Holiday Fair	£200 per day	January
Holiday Fair	Geneva	Consumer Holiday Fair	£200 per day	February
OP PAD Activity Fair	The Hague	Activity Holiday Fair	£200 per day	February **
BIT	Milan	Int'l. Trade and Consumer Fair	£400 for stand	February **
European Trade Workshop	Dublin	Meetings between tour operators and tourism providers	£220 per day	May **
Mitcar	Paris	Coach Operators Fair	£800 per stand	October **
World Travel Market (WTM)	London	Int'l Travel Trade Fair	£550 per day	November

** These trade fairs were attended by North Clare LEADER Tourism during 1993/4.

EXHIBIT 18: IRISH COUNTRY HOLIDAYS — PERFORMANCE OF MARKETING ACTIVITIES 1992 -1994

Bednights Booked:
1992 292
1993 3,400
1994 10,500 (plus 32,000 locally)

Trade Relations:
1992 2-3 Agents
1993 20 Agents featuring in brochures
1994 30 Agents featuring in brochures
1994 10 Agents working with central office.

Cost Of Employing Marketing Executive = £20,000 per annum.

Contribution per Community Group (13 groups) as at December 1994 = £1,538.

EXHIBIT 19: IRISH COUNTRY HOLIDAYS — SPECIFICATIONS OF A RURAL TOURISM HOLIDAY

Apart from the opportunity to sample open, free, fresh unpolluted countryside and scenery and the friendliness of the Irish people, the key elements of an "Irish Country Holidays" package were:

1. Accommodation in farmhouse or town and country homes.
2. Admittance to a working family farm with refreshments.
3. Admittance to a day visitor attraction in each region visited e.g. heritage centre, tour of archaeological site, boat ride on a lake.
4. An "Irish Coffee" on the final evening with the host families.
5. An information pack containing details of all items, places of interest in the region, a welcoming letter with name of guest, an evaluation sheet and freepost envelope, which clients are encouraged to fill, and two pass tickets for visits to open farm and day visitor attractions.

An inter-community package was available if a client prefered to stay in three co-op areas over a seven-day stay.

Source: Irish Country Holidays, 1995.

EXHIBIT 20: PRODUCT SPECIFICATIONS — IRISH COUNTRY HOLIDAY MEMBER ORGANISATIONS

1. All accommodation must be approved by Bord Failte
2. Recommended minimum catchment area is 15 miles radius from centre of the region.
3. A minimum of 120 beds must be available, 75 per cent of which must be Farmhouse or Countryhouse accommodation.
4. Day Visitor attractions, Open Farms etc. must be available for each I.C.H. client.
5. A tourism information pack must be available for each I.C.H. client.

6. It is essential that agreement on pricing be adhered to within the co-operative.
7. The group must have adequate public liability insurance.
8. All activities must be registered and approved by the relevant body e.g. A.I.R.E. for Equestrian.
9. It is essential that each group have a co-ordinator with a minimum requirement of Office, Telephone and Fax.

Source: Irish Country Holidays, 1995.

EXHIBIT 21: MARKETING BUDGETS FROM RURAL RESOURCE DEVELOPMENTS UNDER LEADER 1

Clare West LEADER	£60,000
Clare East LEADER	£50,000
Clare Mid LEADER	£29,500
North Clare LEADER	£101,000

EXHIBIT 22: VISITORS' QUESTIONNAIRE

North Clare LEADER Tourism Promotions
Enterprise Centre, Lisdoonvarna, Co. Clare, Ireland.
Tel: 065-74580/74603. Fax 065-74581.

1. What country are you from?______________________________

2. How did you hear about North Clare?

   Travel Agency/Tour Operator ❑
   Brochure ❑
   Friends/Family ❑
   Other ______________________________________

3. If staying in the region, where:

Hotel	❑	Town & Country Home	❑
Farmhouse	❑	Guesthouse	❑
Hostel	❑	Self Catering	❑
Camping/Caravan	❑	Friends/Family	❑
Just passing through	❑		

4. Length of stay, number of nights____________________

5. Do you intend pursuing any of the following activities while you are on holiday?

Bird Watching	❑	Cycling	❑
Diving	❑	Fishing	❑
Golf	❑	Painting	❑
The Burren	❑	Walking	❑

Other ____

Name:____

Address:____

Comments:____

____

EXHIBIT 23: PRODUCT PROVIDERS' QUESTIONNAIRE

In order to assist the new board of North Clare LEADER Tourism Promotions [N.C.L.T.P.], to plan a strategy for the promotion of tourism throughout North Clare, you are requested to complete this brief questionnaire.

[Please tick appropriate box or add comments where relevant].
****

1. One of the main aims of N.C.L.T.P. is to market North Clare as a traditional area with special emphasis on special interest holidays, such as walking and cycling. Do you agree that this is the correct approach?

   Yes ❑ No ❑ Don't know ❑

Comments/Suggestions:

2. A range of literature has been produced by N.C.L.T.P. to promote the area. Are you satisfied with the quality and content of this literature?

   Yes ❑ No❑ Don't know ❑

Comments/Suggestions:

3. N.C.L.T.P. has attended trade fairs in several European countries where contact has been made with many tourism promoters. Do you think that this type of marketing is worthwhile?
   Yes ❑ No ❑ Don't know ❑

Comments/Suggestions:

4. Some marketing has taken place in Ireland. Are you satisfied with the efforts in this regard?
   Yes ❑ No ❑ Don't know ❑

Comments/Suggestions:

5. Another aim of N.C.L.T.P. has been to provide detailed information to tourists in each town and village in North Clare. Do you feel that the provision of local tourist information points has been successful?
   Yes ❑ No ❑ Don't know ❑

Comments/Suggestions:

6. In your opinion, is it possible to make local tourist information points, self-financing?
   Yes ❑ No ❑ Don't know ❑

Comments/Suggestions:

7. In your opinion, is there a practical mechanism for monitoring the number of bednights generated by N.C.L.T.P. initiatives in North Clare?
   Yes ❑ No ❑ Don't know ❑

Comments/Suggestions:

8. An administrative office for N.C.L.T.P. has operated at Lisdoonvarna for almost two years. Do you feel that this office has been of benefit to tourism operations in North Clare?
   Yes ❑ No ❑ Don't know ❑

Comments/Suggestions:

9. As a tourism operator in the area, have you been kept informed of the activities of N.C.L.T.P. on a regular basis?

    Yes ❑ No ❑ Don't know ❑

Comments/Suggestions:

10. N.C.L.T.P. has been mostly funded through a LEADER grant matched by the voluntary effort of the committee as well as contributions from tourism operators. Comparatively speaking do you feel that your contribution was value for money?

    Yes ❑ No ❑ Don't know ❑

Comments/Suggestions:

11. N.C.L.T.P. has worked closely with other community tourism initiatives in the other areas of the county. In the long term do you feel that North Clare would be better served by marketing all of Clare as one unit?

    Yes ❑ No ❑ Don't know ❑

Comments/Suggestions:

12. N.C.L.T.P. has been involved in the provision of a number of tourism related training courses, such as computers, languages, agri-tourism, etc. Do you feel that this has been a positive development?

    Yes ❑ No ❑ Don't know ❑

Comments/Suggestions:

13. N.C.L.T.P. has come in for public criticism from some quarters. In your opinion has this criticism been justified?

    Yes ❑ No ❑ Don't know ❑

Comments/Suggestions:

Please include any other observations or recommendations you might have which you feel are important to developing and promoting tourism in North Clare.

EXHIBIT 24: RESULTS OF PRODUCT PROVIDERS' SURVEY

Response to Subscriber Questionnaire Re Marketing Activities

Q. No	*Yes*	*No*	*Don't know*	*Question Topic*
1	88.5%	8%	3.5%	Traditional Activities
2	84.5%	4%	11.5%	Range of literature
3	84.5%	4%	11.5%	Trade Fairs
4	46%	23%	31%	Home Marketing
5	92%	8%	0%	T.I.P.s
6	23%	42%	35%	Self-financing T.I.P.s
7	23%	31%	46%	Practical Bednight Monitoring
8	58%	15.5%	22.5%	Admin. office beneficial
9	54%	38%	8%	Regular info. from N.C.L.T.
10	81%	15.5%	3.5%	Value for Money
11	46%	50%	4%	Marketing Co. Clare as a unit
12	84.5%	4%	11.5%	Education
13	23%	23%	54%	Justified Criticism

5

MITSUBISHI ELECTRIC IRELAND LTD[1]

John Fahy

INTRODUCTION

"Cola Wars: Its the Real Thing". As he relaxed over a cup of coffee one morning, Fergus Madigan was drawn to this headline in the business section of a Sunday newspaper. The editorial went on to describe how the traditional big brands seemed to be under attack and not even such bastions as Coca-Cola and Kellogg's Corn Flakes seemed to be safe. The world of marketing it appeared was being turned on its head and the correspondent wondered if it would ever be the same again. Marlboro Friday, diaper Tuesday and cola Thursday. These rumblings of the stock markets illustrated that attacks on big brands by new competitors was having a serious impact on the share prices of consumer goods giants such as Philip Morris, Proctor and Gamble and Coca Cola. Aside from nimble competitors like Virgin, the central point of attack appeared to be from major distributors, who due to their increasing power were able to launch their own brands to compete with the traditional manufacturer's brand. It seemed to reflect what many commentators had been forecasting, which was that there would continue to be a powershift from manufacturers to retailers in the marketing channel.

The article struck a chord with Fergus Madigan, managing director of Mitsubishi Electric Ireland (MEIR), who had overseen the strong growth of Mitsubishi products on the Irish market. His

[1] This case is intended to serve as a basis for class discussion rather than to show either effective or ineffective management. The author gratefully acknowledges the assistance and support of the management staff at Mitsubishi Electric Ireland Ltd., and the contribution of a Trinity MBA project group in the collection of the data.

company had always subscribed to the importance of brand building and now had a brand name that was both well known and associated with high quality, technologically advanced products. But he had noticed the home entertainment business in Ireland was undergoing a fundamental transformation. Not least among the changes was the emergence of a powerful group of discount chains following similar patterns in the US and other developed nations. These chains seemed to have the capability to threaten consumer electronics firms in similar ways to which some food retailers were challenging the leading food and drinks companies. As he reflected on the plight of some of the world's biggest brand names, Fergus Madigan's thoughts began to turn to the implications these trends were likely to have for the home entertainment business in Ireland.

THE HOME ENTERTAINMENT INDUSTRY

The home entertainment business had grown dramatically throughout the developed world since the end of the second World War and appeared to be on the crest of another revolution. Home entertainment comprised a range of audio products (radio, stereo, compact and mini discs and compact cassettes), video products (VCR, TV, cable, satellite and camcorders) and interactive products such as computer games and "smart boxes". The market for TVs and VCRs had reached saturation point in many developed countries. Competition for market share became intense and leading firms in the industry such as Sanyo and Philips had suffered losses (see world market share data, Exhibit 1). Other firms responded by developing multiple extensions of their basic product lines. For example, in 1994, Sony went as far as launching a water resistant television designed specifically for use in bathrooms.

The home entertainment industry was on the verge of a technological revolution. For example, the television had been a relatively stable product, remaining essentially the same since its introduction in the 1930s. Analogue signals, transmitted by cable or antenna, were converted by the set into electrons and sprayed onto the picture tube. Since standards for broadcast TV were set in the 1950s, the only major change has been the addition of colour capability (CTV). However, a worldwide race to introduce a new form of high definition television (HDTV) appeared to have been won by the United States. In February 1994, the US announced a new digital HDTV standard formulated by a "grand alliance" of high-tech companies, including the two biggest European TV manufacturers, Philips and Thomson GE/RCA. Europe's own HDTV analogue standard development (HD-MAC) had been abandoned in 1993 and the US digital version was perceived to be superior to the Japanese analogue HDTV, though the latter persisted with developing their own standard.

The implications of digital transmission, however, extended well beyond HDTV applications. Digital technology, whereby any form of information (text, graphics, sound, video images) can be coded as a series of binary digits, had several advantages over analogue technology. Firstly, the coded information could be reproduced more accurately than through analogue transmission, with the result that colours and patterns were crisper and clearer. Secondly, digital signals could be compressed allowing for various kinds of information to travel on the same channel which opened up possibilities for interactive multi-media. Finally, digitalisation ended the necessity for real-time transmission, in other words, an hour's worth of programming could be delivered in seconds. Digital compact cassettes for video, digital stereo sound and digital satellite transmission were some of the innovations being developed in Europe.

A variety of firms not traditionally considered part of the home entertainment industry were likely to have a significant impact on its future. Computer manufacturers such as Sega, Sun Microsystems and IBM were working on "smart boxes" which facilitated interactive television. Matsushita, Philips and Sony were partners with General Magic, a software consortium, while Microsoft and Intel also formed an alliance in the race to develop interactive TV. One of the possibilities provided by interactive television is the concept of "movies on demand" which threatened to obliterate the traditional video rental industry. At the same time a number of telecommunications companies had invested in cable firms in order to develop strong market positions with regard to digital technology opportunities.

THE HOME ENTERTAINMENT INDUSTRY IN IRELAND

Ireland, in line with most other economies in the Western world, had a well-developed market of home entertainment products. In 1994, 98 per cent of Irish households had at least one television set and 96 per cent of these were colour sets. Ownership of VCRs had grown to almost 60 per cent of all households (See Figure 1 for ownership levels of TV and VCR products).

FIGURE 1: OWNERSHIP OF TV AND VCR PRODUCTS, 1994

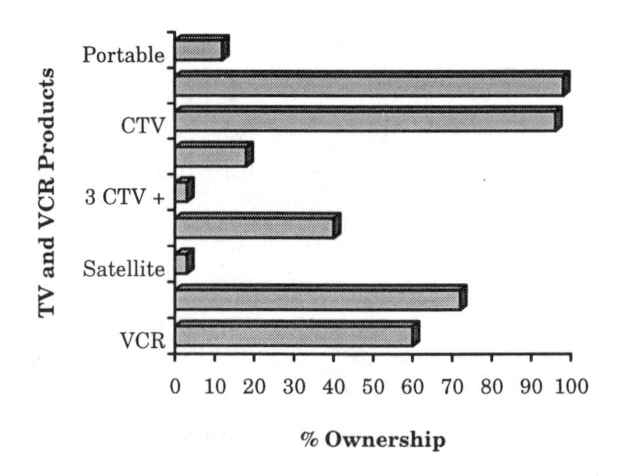

Ownership of TVs and VCRs was higher in urban households than in either urban apartments or rural households. Differences in ownership were less dramatic across age groups though the highest proportion of VCR owners are in the 18-35 age group. The average life of a television set was 5-7 years. Recent research indicated that some 25 per cent of the Irish market had purchased their main TV in the past three years indicating a strong replacement demand. This demand was particularly pronounced in the younger age groups and urban segments (See Exhibit 2).

Some notable trends had emerged in terms of product features and pricing of TVs and VCRs. In terms of screen size, demand was strongest for large screen TVs (greater than 27 inches) and for small screen TVs (14-15 inches) reflecting purchases of small second or third TVs as well as an upgrading of the main household TV. Demand for TVs with features such as Nicam stereo and

Teletext was also growing with the latter rising to 27 per cent in 1994. With regard to VCRs however, the demand for extra features such as Video Plus, long-play action and Nicam stereo had been less brisk with the majority of products sold being less sophisticated, two head systems with standard play action and mono sound. These patterns suggested that the Irish market is lagging behind other countries where there was a growing trend towards "home theatre systems" encompassing large screen TVs, a Dolby surround sound system, a laser disc player and VCR, with greater user control. In terms of pricing, the early 1990s were characterised by a period of stagnant or falling prices. However, 1994, had seen some upward movement reflecting the emergence from recession and the demand for more sophisticated products in line with trends in Europe generally.

DISTRIBUTION

Distribution was managed almost exclusively through direct contact with retailers. Wholesalers, while they were present in Ireland, accounted for only 3 per cent of total TV/VCR sales. Electrical goods retailers in Ireland could broadly be categorised as brown goods specialists, white goods specialists or combination dealers (general electric shops, department stores) (See Table 1).

TABLE 1: DEALER SIZE BY TYPE

Shop Type	*Small*	*Large*
	(Turnover less than IR£250,000)	(Turnover greater than IR£250,000)
Brown	47%	53%
White	33%	67%
Combination Dealer	50%	50%

Brown goods were audio-visual products such as TVs and VCRs, while white goods referred to domestic appliances such as refrigerators, cookers and so on. Specialist dealers were those for whom 60 per cent of their sales were either brown or white goods. Some one-third of white goods specialists carried home entertainment products. These shops were expected to broaden their product range with an average of 6 per cent each year expected to begin stocking brown goods. The total market for brown goods in Ireland was estimated to be IR£140 million in 1994.

The rental market in Ireland had been declining in line with trends throughout Europe. Between 1990 and 1991, rental of TVs declined by 3 per cent, while that of VCRs fell by a substantial 11 per cent. The rental market was an important one for white goods specialists accounting for some 50 per cent of all TVs/VCRs disposed in contrast with only 20 per cent for brown goods specialists (See Exhibit 3). Repair services were also an important source of revenue in the industry accounting for on average about 10 per cent of sales. Ninety-two per cent of brown goods specialists and 76 per cent of combination dealers provided repair services. However, this source of revenue was threatened by an increasing propensity among manufacturers to service their own products.

Each of the major manufacturers had varying degrees of success in their penetration of the alternate channels in Ireland. In the distribution of TVs and VCRs, Panasonic and Sony relied heavily on brown goods specialists, Sharp relied on white goods specialists, while Philips had secured high levels of penetration in both white goods outlets and combination dealers. Mitsubishi had also successfully developed a dual distribution channel with strong coverage of both brown goods and combination dealers (See Figure 2).

In 1989, Ireland had some 522 independent dealers (higher per capita than any other EC country) accounting for 84 per cent of total turnover. However, since then the number of electrical outlets in Ireland had declined at a rate of 10-15 per cent per year and the market was becoming increasingly concentrated. Large discounters had several advantages which made them a serious threat to the independent retailers. They carried a wide range of products in every segment of the TV/VCR market and could avail of economies of scale in buying operations that allowed them to retail these products at highly competitive prices. They were concentrated primarily in large urban areas but offered nationwide sales and service through telephone ordering and free delivery. Finally, in their suburban locations these discounters maintained longer opening hours and could easily facilitate Sunday shopping. Equally, the independent dealers were at a competitive disadvantage *vis-à-vis* the Electricity Supply Board (ESB), the state electricity company. Its network of some 100 shops offered customers a unique form of financing whereby instalment payments were attached to utility bills.

FIGURE 2: PERCENTAGE OF CTV BRAND DISTRIBUTION BY CHANNEL

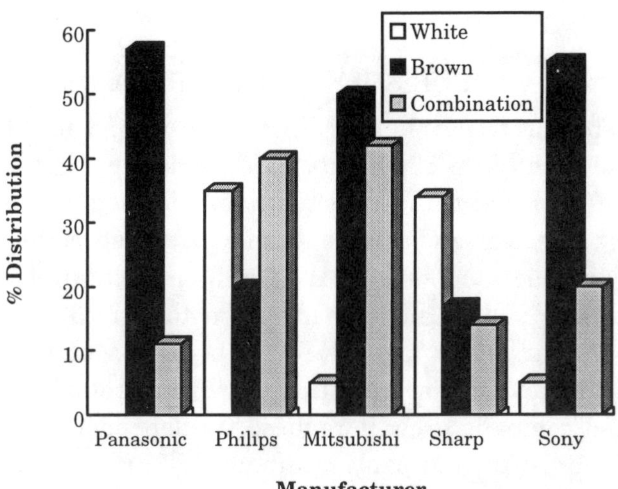

Concentration of the market reflected international patterns where, for example, in the US consumer electronic superstores offered zero percentage financing, extended warranties and toll-free service. The growth of such superstores in Europe was assisted by new regulations which allowed parallel importing of consumer electronics products. This increased the feasibility of distributors deciding to service the complete European market from a single base, taking the concept of scale and volume to a new level. A distributor in the UK, Argos, was pursuing this strategy operating with very low overheads and devoting minimum resources to sales staff and merchandising. Careful use of information technology afforded these kinds of firms the opportunity to telemarket their products on a pan-European basis.

The relationships which manufacturers maintained with these different groups of dealers varied significantly. Small independent shops employed a strategy of carrying a limited range of brands which were tailored carefully to their local markets. Manufacturers with strong brands negotiated arrangements with independent dealers whereby certain products (which a dealer felt were necessary for success) would only be supplied if certain other products were bought as well. However, the position of the manufacturer was somewhat weaker with regard to the discount chains as the latter's volume of sales put them in a stronger bargaining position.

MITSUBISHI ELECTRIC IRELAND

Mitsubishi Electric Ireland (MEIR) was opened in 1981 as the Dublin branch office of Mitsubishi Electric UK. The initial staff consisted of a managing director, two salesmen, an accountant, secretary, engineer and a warehouse logistics specialist. Together this group generated sales of IR£1 million in its first year of operations. By 1982, turnover had grown to IR£4.5 million and a mere four years after opening, MEIR became a market leader in sales of TVs and VCRs, a position that it has retained (See Table 2). As the company grew it reduced its dependence on TVs and VCRs. In 1984, the company set up an OEM unit to meet the demand coming from the computer industry for disk drives, monitors and circuit protection products. In 1985, an industrial unit was established to meet the needs of industrial customers for energy saving motor components such as programmable logic controllers and inverters. In recent years a variety of other products have been added including security products, air conditioning, facsimile and cellular phone ranges. TVs and VCRs now account for less than 50 per cent of MEIR's annual turnover.

TABLE 2: MANUFACTURER'S SHARE OF TV AND VCR — IRELAND

Manufacturer	*1991*	*1992*	*1993*
Market Share — TVs	%	%	%
Mitsubishi Electric	22	20	22
Philips	17	19	19
Sanyo	14	16	14
Thomson/Ferguson	6	5	8
Sony	8	8	7
Grundig	8	6	7
Salora	6	6	6

Panasonic	8	5	5
Blaupunkt	0	1	5
Market Share — VCRs	%	%	%
Mitsubishi Electric	24	26	28
Philips	15	19	17
Sanyo	12	11	14
Matsushita	14	10	10
Thomson/Ferguson	5	6	8
JVC	8	6	7
Salora	8	7	5
Sony	8	6	5
Grundig	6	4	3

MEIR is one of the 106 subsidiaries and affiliates of the Mitsubishi Electric Corporation located in over 90 countries. The corporation operated a dual reporting system so MEIR reported to both its head office in the UK as well as the corporate office in Tokyo. Other than this reporting obligation, MEIR operated autonomously in Ireland, which allowed it to be flexible in response to changing conditions. However, its scope was restricted by its dependence on its Japanese parent as a source of supply for new products. In keeping with its Japanese ethos, MEIR placed a great deal of emphasis on gaining long-term market share rather than on achieving short-term profitability. Indeed, it has become highly regarded within the corporation as it was the only branch which had achieved the number one market share position in its local market and its branding capability was regarded as a significant strength. Its unofficial but well-articulated vision, spearheaded by the managing director and embraced by MEIR management and staff, was quite simply to be the best: best in terms of customer satisfaction, best in terms of distribution management, best in terms of perceived brand value and best in terms of market share. This was reflected in the company's three-tier strategy which was to maintain a good distribution network, to maintain a strong brand and to carefully position its product line. Its primary objective was to grow sales annually by 10 per cent through to 1997. Given the saturation in the TV and VCR markets this meant a need to focus attention on the importance of new products.

Company Structure

The structure of the organisation is illustrated in Exhibit 4. It had three distinct business units to deal with each of its key constituents, namely, the consumer market, the industrial market and the OEM market. Each operated to pre-set budgets and were evaluated in terms of gross margins. Overhead and indirect costs were allocated according to company objectives and a considerable amount of cross-subsidisation took place between the units. The strategies of each were co-ordinated with overall company goals.

In addition to the three operating units the company had separate corporate marketing and technical support units. Corporate marketing had responsibility for servicing the other operating units as well as the customer support process. This process tracked every order from entry to dispatch and was designed to reflect the company's fanatical approach to customer service. Incoming customer calls were fed into an exchange. From there, they were automatically routed to the first free line in the customer support group. Orders were taken and once the necessary price and credit checks were made, the relevant operating unit was contacted to arrange delivery within 48 hours. Customer complaints were logged and forwarded to the relevant department for handling. One consequence of this system was that all incoming calls were treated with equal priority irrespective of whether the caller was a small retailer or a major OEM customer. Equally, it did not allow for any specialisation within the customer support group and the system tended to come under pressure at the peak times such as November and December each year.

The technical support and quality control function consisted of the warehouse, inventory control and technical laboratory. The laboratory provided both product testing and repair capabilities as well as customer and product feedback to MEIR through questionnaires that dealers filled out when repair work was done. The manager of this group monitored both the physical movement of goods in and out of the warehouse and company adherence to ISO quality standards.

Corporate responsibility was shared between the managing director and the general manager with the former holding ultimate authority. The managing director was responsible for the firm's external activities, primarily sales and marketing as well as sitting on a number of committees in the UK headquarters. The general manager oversaw the day-to-day running of the operation with responsibility for the finance/accounting and human resource management, the latter with which he was assisted by an outside consultant.

Marketing Strategy

The central plank of the company's marketing strategy had been the development of a strong brand image. Its dedication to the concept of branding was the guiding principle in all its promotion, from its simplest press coverage to its most extensive advertising campaigns. As a result, MEIR had been able to command a premium position in the marketplace which in turn allowed it to maximise its margins and profit potential.

The company devoted 5 per cent of its sales to brand development. This budget was based on sales forecasts rather than sales revenues, thus ensuring that brand support was not reduced during "bad years". Brand development took place at both the corporate and product levels. At the corporate level, the focus was on developing an image of the Mitsubishi name that was associated with a large, technologically advanced manufacturer of quality products. It also sought to demonstrate that it was a community-oriented company by including leading sports personalities such as Ronnie Delaney, an Olympic gold medalist, and Ronnie Whelan, an Irish soccer international, in its advertising. The company name was promoted through participation in community events as well as through the standard advertising media such as national newspapers and billboards.

At the product level, promotion centred on particular products which reflected state-of-the-art technology. This was achieved through co-operative advertising with dealers and consumer promotions such as rebates and discounts based on purchases made. Co-operative advertising was designed to provide incentives for dealers and proved particularly beneficial to small independent retailers who often lacked sophisticated promotion capability. The aim of consumer promotions, aside from simply selling products, was to promote their particular features. By emphasising specific attributes, MEIR strengthened the general perception of Mitsubishi products as high quality and technologically advanced.

One of the perpetual problem's for MEIR, given its budget confines, was the balancing of its corporate marketing and product marketing activities which traditionally had been given an equal portion of the promotion budget. However, a shifting emphasis given to these is illustrated in Figure 3. In part the change from 1993 to 1994 can be explained by opportunities offered by Ireland's qualification for the 1994 Soccer World Cup. MEIR had a contract with the manager of the Irish team, Jack Charlton, who was engaged primarily in their corporate promotions and to a lesser extent in trade marketing such as visits to top performing dealers. This promotion had been very effective in generating direct business during the World Cup when MEIR offered large screen TVs to public house owners at a discount in a joint-promotion with Guinness Ireland.

FIGURE 3: CHANGING BRAND STRATEGY EMPHASIS, 1993-94

Promotion Component	*1993 (%)*	*1994 (%)*
Corporate Branding	30	65
Co-operative Advertising	50	25
Consumer Promotions	20	10

Research conducted by MEIR indicated that it had been very successful in its brand-building efforts in Ireland. In terms of awareness, and pitted against some well established rivals, recognition of the Mitsubishi name — which had initially been difficult for Irish consumers to pronounce — had grown as high as 87 per cent in just 13 years. In terms of quality, Mitsubishi products were perceived by the consumer to be the highest by a wide margin and it was also the brand that most consumers automatically associated with Nicam Stereo Sound Televisions, which was arguably the single biggest advance in television technology since the advent of colour. However, the company recognised that this brand franchise faced a new challenge in the future with the growing concentration of the distribution channel.

CHANNEL MANAGEMENT: A NEW COMPETITIVE CHALLENGE

The nucleus of MEIR's dealer base could be traced back to the managing director and the relationships he had developed before forming the company. It targeted dealers that it had identified as being the strongest in local areas in the country for a projected portfolio of 100 in total. Rather than sell Mitsubishi products through unsuitable dealers, the company took a long-term view and began the process of developing both its product and company image. It created an atmosphere of exclusivity whereby only the most successful dealers in an area were given the opportunity to sell Mitsubishi products. Thus, a "club" atmosphere was developed which created dealer demand for the product. This was reinforced by a strong package of dealer benefits which further developed the relationship. The package consisted of incentives, training, advertising support and marketing expertise intended to both reward the dealers and make them more competitive.

MEIR had five classes of dealers ranked on the basis of annual turnover. Class AA were the biggest consisting of accounts with an annual turnover of IR£200,000. Class A accounts had a turnover of between IR£100,000 and IR£199,000, Class B a turnover of IR£60,000 to IR£99,000, Class C a turnover of IR£20,000 to IR£59,000 and Class D a turnover of less than IR£19,000. (See Table 3). In 1993, the 48 dealers in the top three classes accounted for 90 per cent of total revenue while the 68 dealers in classes C and D accounted for the remaining 10 per cent of revenue. In terms of profit contribution, the pattern was somewhat different. Because of their competitive pricing patterns, sales through larger dealers typically resulted in smaller profit margins to MEIR. This profit pattern was also influenced by the fact that support for dealers declined with their importance. For example, though Class D dealers were characterised by low turnover, they were also the least expensive to manage, not receiving any support from MEIR and paying for products on a cash-on-delivery basis.

TABLE 3: REVENUE CONTRIBUTION BY CLASS

	Revenue Contribution Over Time (%)				
Class	**1993**	**1992**	**1991**	**1990**	**1989**
Class AA	68.23	58.09	49.26	55.0	50.0
Class A	10.10	12.05	13.64	19.0	24.0
Class B	11.72	13.08	14.93	12.0	13.0
Class C	7.67	10.38	11.72	9.0	4.0
Class D	2.29	5.80	10.44	2.0	4.0

Over the five-year period since 1989 there had been some significant movement within the dealer classes. In all cases there was a familiar pattern where some dealers move up or down between the categories to be replaced by others moving in the opposite direction. Class AA accounts consisted of discount chains, large independents and department stores. Most new AAs were previously in the A class though a major discount chain, Power City, started as an AA account. In 1993, 55 per cent of AA accounts had been in this class for more than five years. There had been a significant overall drop in Class A dealers from 23 to 10 since 1989. A small number developed into AA accounts with the majority falling to B, C and D levels. Of the ten A accounts in 1993, 70 per cent had been in this category for at least five years.

The B class had traditionally provided the biggest margins to MEIR. The number of B accounts rose in 1993 though the profit contribution of this group remained relatively stable suggesting that the average B account was becoming smaller. Movements in the C class were greater than in any of the other classes. Twenty-eight per cent of accounts had been in this class for at least four years, while only 3 per cent had been there for more than five years. Similarly, the number of D accounts had grown by over 200 per cent since 1989. The revenue contribution of this group had declined significantly since 1991, implying that the average account had become smaller (see Table 4).

The growth in the lower classes indicated that either previously strong dealers were unable to fully adapt to the increasingly competitive environment or that they had been promoting other brands at the expense of the Mitsubishi brand. In either case, it indicated that a large proportion of MEIR's dealer portfolio had been decreasing their level of business with MEIR.

TABLE 4: NUMBER OF DEALERS PER CLASS (1899-1993)

Class	*1993*	*1992*	*1991*	*1990*	*1989*
Class AA	19	17	13	19	18
Class A	10	19	26	20	23
Class B	19	11	13	21	23
Class C	29	35	30	27	12
Class D	39	33	31	28	19

MANAGING THE DISTRIBUTION CHANNEL

Conscious of the trends taking place in the market, the managing director decided to conduct an audit of the distribution channel. Sales patterns were analysed and discussions were held with channel members to solicit their views. From this research the following strategic alternatives appeared to be available to the company.

A. Reduce the Number of Channel Members

The analysis of distribution revealed that a very high proportion of dealers provided little in the way of revenues and profits to the company. Nineteen class AA dealers contributed almost 70 per cent of revenue while 68 class C and D dealers combined contributed less than 10 per cent. MEIR could decide to remove these two classes from its portfolio and concentrate solely on the larger players enabling them to provide a better service to this strengthening group.

B. Provide a Level Playing Field

Discussions with the company's dealers yielded evidence of some dissatisfaction with recent trends. The marketplace had become increasingly competitive, margins were eroding and many dealers felt that brown good specialists had very little future in the industry. With specific reference to MEIR, there was some dissatisfaction too as many dealers felt that the notion of the exclusive "club" of which they once felt part seemed to have disappeared. MEIR now had some 116 dealers nationwide, but more significantly, there was a feeling that not all dealers were being treated equally. MEIR had always pursued the traditional Japanese practice of negotiating individually and privately with each dealer. The result of this was that there was little uniformity of business terms among dealers, to the extent that an aggressive B account dealer could gain better terms than a larger A account dealer. At the bottom end of the scale, the smaller independent brown goods specialist was being forced to operate on a cash-on-delivery basis while at the same time large discount chains were able to avail of exclusive promotions. Exclusive promotions like these, it was felt, eroded the premium image of the brand. At the same time, it created disquiet among dealers who felt hamstrung in their efforts to compete with the discount chains and became much more sensitive to marginal differences in the terms being offered to other dealers. They proposed that all dealers be allowed to begin at the same starting point which would enable them to compete more effectively with the larger discount chains thus stalling the latter's growing power in the marketplace.

The idea of a level playing field left MEIR with two options. One, it could seek to level the playing field for all its dealers by instituting a policy of recommended resale prices and national consumer promotions which would be advertised in the national media. This could be backed by a standard approach to co-operative advertising or all co-operative advertising could cease with the money saved moving to consumer promotions. Alternatively, MEIR could seek to re-institute the notion of a club or clubs by tailoring sales terms to each class ensuring that members of the same class were given the same terms.

C. Work Closely with Dealers

Market research in the industry demonstrated that the dealers' salespeople were an important player in the consumer buying decision. It revealed that the salesperson rated higher than brand awareness, promotion and brand loyalty in influencing purchasing decisions. This was accentuated by a low level of brand loyalty in the industry despite high levels of brand recognition. For example, while awareness of the Mitsubishi name was as high as 87 per cent its market share for televisions in 1993 was 22 per cent. This implies that its ratio of brand loyalty to brand awareness was approximately one-quarter. Salespeople had the ability to convince customers to switch brands by highlighting particular features of the product and actively demonstrating these during a customer's visit to the shop. Inevitably, the brands a salesperson was likely to promote were going to be influenced by how he or she is motivated to promote the brand.

Trade promotions in the industry, such as free trips were typically aimed at store owners and not the sales staff. This again presented MEIR with two possible approaches. It could focus on directly providing incentives for salespeople in its dealerships. This would involve replacing the current package of free trips with a system that directly links points earned by the sales staff with the number of MEIR products sold. The points accumulated could directly relate to the cumulative value of each of the products sold, with top margin items earning more points. These accumulated points could then be exchanged for holiday trips arranged by MEIR in a fashion similar to the frequent flyer programmes adopted by airlines. Alternatively, it could introduce a comprehensive package of sales training for the salespeople. The objective of this approach would be to create salesperson loyalty and to better equip them, in terms of technical knowledge and selling skills, to promote and sell MEIR products. Such training seminars would have the advantage of allowing MEIR staff to make direct contact with dealer salespeople, presenting a vehicle for transmitting its way of doing business as well as mechanisms for collecting market information and for training sales people in the proper use of Mitsubishi products and promotional material.

D. Increase its Level of Direct Business

Its very successful direct promotion with Guinness Ireland and Irish public house owners during the 1994 Soccer World Cup had demonstrated to MEIR the potential available in direct sales. This joint promotion benefited all the parties concerned. MEIR was able to take advantage of the demand at the time for large screen televisions and to significantly increase its volume of sales of this high value product. Guinness Ireland was able to enhance its relationships with the publicans by providing zero-percent financing for the purchases. MEIR dealers then delivered and installed these pre-sold products for the publican though at somewhat reduced margins for themselves. Generally, an increasing proportion of MEIR's revenue had been becoming from this kind of direct business.

Thinking ahead to next Monday's monthly review of operations, Fergus Madigan pondered on the choices available to the company. He wondered which approach or combinations of approaches might be most effective in the long term but as well he wanted to be sure that there were not any other options that he had as yet failed to consider.

EXHIBIT 1: MARKET SHARES FOR TVS AND VCRS IN LEADING MARKETS

	Television		*VCR*
US (1990)			
Thomson GE/RCA	21	Matsushita	21
Philips (US)	13	Thomson GE/RCA	15
Zenith	12	Philips	9
Sony	7	Emerson	9
Matsushita	6	Sharp	7
Sanyo/Fisher	5	JVC	5
Japan (1991)			
Matsushita	22.5	Matsushita	28.6
Toshiba	14.5	Victor Co. (Japan)	16.7
Sharp	14.5	Mitsubishi	15.3
Hitachi	10.5	Toshiba	12
Sony	10.5	Sharp	8.7
Europe (1992)			
Philips	13.4		
Grundig	9.7		
Sony	8.8		
Telefunken	4.1		
Sanyo	2.8		
Samsung	2.7		
Matsushita	2.5		
Toshiba	2.4		
Sharp	2.4		
Hitachi	2.2		

EXHIBIT 2: THE IRISH TV/VCR MARKET

	Purchasing Patterns		
Age Group	Average TV Sets/Household	% Ownership of VCRs	% Acquiring Main TV in Last Three Years
18-25	1.5	24	26
26-49	1.6	20	27
50-59	1.4	25	21
60+	1.2	13	20
Household Type			
Urban House	1.7	25	30
Urban Apartment	1.0	22	11
Rural House	1.3	18	20

EXHIBIT 3: PERCENTAGE OF PRODUCTS DISPOSED THROUGH RETAIL

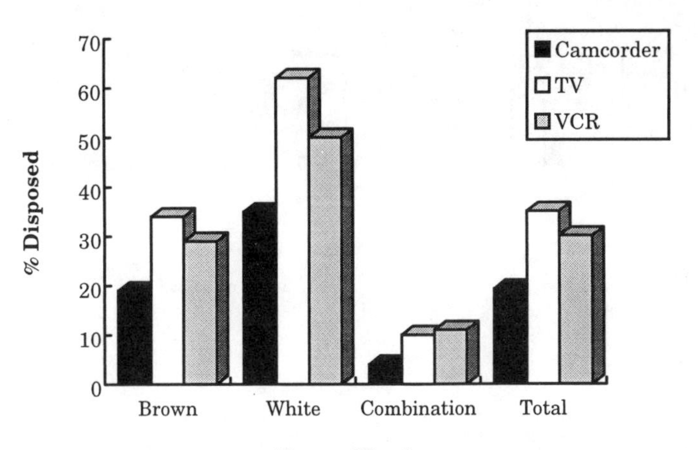

EXHIBIT 4: COMPANY STRUCTURE OF MITSUBISHI ELECTRIC IRELAND (MEIR)

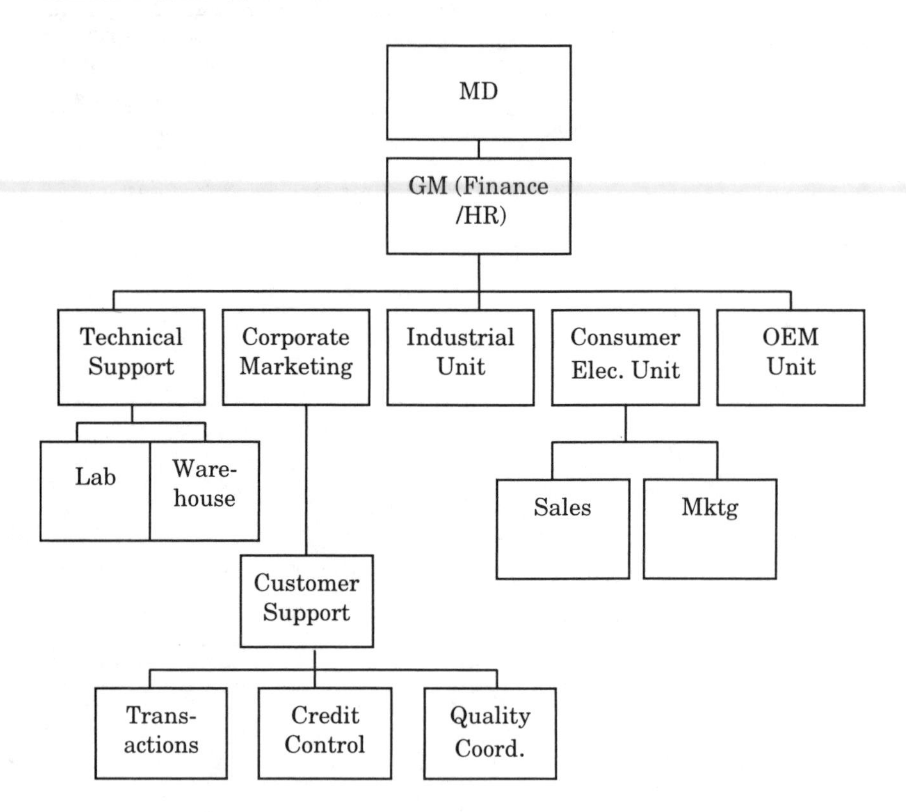

6

MONAGHAN MUSHROOMS[1]

Barra O Cinneide

INTRODUCTION

Co. Monaghan, situated in the North East of the Republic of Ireland, is one of the country's smallest counties in terms of size and population. It borders Northern Ireland and retains many features of the traditional culture/lifestyle of the historic province of Ulster, of which it is a constituent part. The agricultural holdings, averaging 15-20 hectares, are well below the EU level and the whole of Co. Monaghan has been classified as "disadvantaged" in European Community terms, therefore entitling farmers to maximum support funding for agricultural and regional development. The principal source of income is agriculture — the mainstays of the local economy being dairying and beef production but, traditionally, the county has been a prime contributor, also, to white meat (pig and poultry) production in Ireland. In recent decades, however, the North East of Ireland has become a significant base for horticulture, gearing most of its output to export markets, particularly the United Kingdom. One firm in particular, Monaghan Mushrooms, located at Tyholland, five kilometres from Monaghan town, has been influential in developing this sector of agribusiness activity.

In the early 1980s, against the background of small-sized, marginal farms, a young VEC (Vocational Educational Committee) school teacher in Co. Monaghan, Ronnie Wilson, explored the

[1] This case study was prepared by Barra O Cinneide, College of Business, University of Limerick, Ireland with the intention of providing a basis for class discussion rather than illustrating either good or bad management practices.

potential for developing alternative indigenous enterprises.[2] One of his initial interests concerned the prospects for profitable use of agricultural "waste", e.g. farmyard manure. Ronnie Wilson, without any specialist agricultural or horticultural expertise, decided to establish a new venture in Tyholland that would help to encourage neighbouring farmers to participate in a new initiative which, though run on a private enterprise basis, would rely on community effort. Monaghan Mushrooms Ltd., a wholly owned subsidiary of the Pleroma group, is now one of the leading mushroom companies in the UK/Ireland. By 1995, the enterprise could claim to have created employment for over 1,100 people, on either a full-time or part-time basis (see Table 1 in the Appendices).

Excluding its growing operations, Monaghan Mushrooms maintains a payroll for more than 300 employees, including over 100 dedicated to collection/distribution, 65 in composting operations, more than 50 within the "Fresh Division" and on processing activities, 10 specialist advisors to growers, and up to 90 personnel involved in marketing, administration and management. An organogram, representing the management roles within Monaghan Mushrooms at year end 1993 is contained in Exhibit 1 in the Appendices.

THE IRISH MUSHROOM SECTOR

Pre-1980 the Irish mushroom sector was comprised mainly of a few large production units. Their operations were based on the traditional British system of growing in large wooden trays, stacked four or five high in the cropping houses. The farms were fully self-contained in that, in addition to growing mushrooms, they produced their own compost and each company undertook the task of marketing its own output. These companies were remarkably innovative and enterprising for their time, but they suffered from several serious drawbacks. These included high capital investment and the difficulty of achieving a sufficient quantity of high quality product, together with attendant management problems because of the large-sized units and high labour costs. In

---

[2] O'Kane, P. (1994): "Mushrooming Millions", (Profile/Ronnie Wilson), Business This Week, *The Irish Times,* 14 October, 1994

addition, the concept of individual marketing made it difficult to penetrate the upper end of the market where quality and continuity of supply were essential. These farms were thus in a weak position to compete successfully on the British market, while the home market had proved to be too small to warrant significant further expansion. However, integrated corporate groups, like Monaghan Mushrooms, emerged which began to apply the benefits of R&D (research and development) and "best practice" promoted by Teagasc, the Agriculture and Food Development Authority, while adopting new strategic business approaches.

THE ROLE OF RESEARCH AND DEVELOPMENT

During the 1970s, research workers at the Kinsealy Research Centre of Teagasc, the Irish Agriculture and Food Development Authority, were examining alternative systems of mushroom production. These included the use of plastic bags placed on the floor of insulated plastic tunnels. Every aspect of the system was investigated, including type of compost, size of bags and general crop management. The result was the prototyping and development of a new system of mushroom production suited to Irish circumstances. One of its main features was the low capital cost. This new system proved to be commercially attractive, in that it allowed people with little capital to develop a small mushroom enterprise. From such research activities, and subsequent exploitation, this particular aspect of Irish horticulture has literally "mushroomed"!

The R&D (research and development) undertaken at Teagasc gave rise to the concept of specialist central compost facilities supplying spawned compost to many small "satellite" growing units. Additionally, in order to ensure the new system would function effectively and efficiently, an integrated organisational structure was proposed as the "model", with central marketing of the mushrooms as a critical core activity. The researchers mainly responsible for this innovative thinking at the time were Cathal MacCanna and Jim Flanagan at Kinsealy. The "Kinsealy Model" was successfully commercialised with the adoption of the system described above by a number of entrepreneurs such as Ronnie Wilson of Tyholland, Co. Monaghan, and Pat Walsh of Gorey, Co.

Wexford. They set about constructing compost facilities to the required high standards, arranging networks of small growing units and establishing appropriate marketing systems. This was done with considerable back-up from the research and advisory personnel of the relevant state bodies.

ORIGINS OF MONAGHAN MUSHROOMS

In recent decades, the North East of Ireland has become a significant base for horticulture, gearing most of its output to export markets, particularly the United Kingdom. One firm in particular, Monaghan Mushrooms, has been influential in developing this sector of agribusiness activity and exploiting marketing opportunities in the United Kingdom.

In 1981, Monaghan Mushrooms set up its franchised network of mushroom growers — a group of enterprising small farmers dedicated to production of quality mushrooms. By establishing its satellite system of mushroom production, the Tyholland firm encouraged the participation of neighbouring farmers in the new initiative. The system that evolved fitted very well into the socio-economic structure of Irish agriculture which is mainly based on small farms. Many of these farms, being on marginal land, were looking for a means of supplementing family farm income and the "Kinsealy model" provided such an opportunity, with the relatively low cost of establishing viable small mushroom units. Training in mushroom growing was provided by the advisory services and, within a short time, most of the new growers became technically proficient, while quickly developing their business expertise "on the job". The company's control systems were devised to align as effectively as possible with the growers' commitment to grow and hand pick mushrooms in order to keep pace with market requirements. Monaghan Mushrooms now has a wide range of activities.

COMPOST MANUFACTURE AND THE GROWING PROCESS

All the main players within the Irish mushroom sector have a strong commitment to investment in purpose-built facilities, including coldstores, work areas that are environmentally controlled, packing and labelling machinery, and transportation systems. For instance, in production of one of the basic inputs, compost, advanced technology is employed. Today's composters have developed reliable systems for producing compost to the quality level needed for yielding firm white mushrooms with high dry matter content. As all the inputs of mushroom compost are natural materials, mainly straw and animal manure, there can be significant variations in their nutrient properties. The composters have imposed stringent monitoring of raw materials to ensure that the production processes give a consistent formula and, consequently, reliable results at the individual farm level.

It is claimed by Monaghan Mushrooms that its grower franchise network, using the bag growing system, offers many advantages as it has been designed to ensure:

- The supply of firm white mushrooms with a high dry matter content and long shelf-life
- The dedication of specific growers to selectively harvest mushrooms for individual customers to their specifications and packaging requirements
- The segregated grower network curtails the spread of disease
- The individual quality control of product, with the features of a "cottage industry" environment. Mushrooms are picked when ready, immediately placed in the grower's coldstore, the first link in the "cool chain" distribution system, and
- The flexibility to increase mushroom production as market conditions dictate.

RANGE OF MONAGHAN MUSHROOMS' OPERATIONS

The Tyholland plant is the focus for "adding value", either through the "Fresh Division" or within processing operations, (e.g. canning). Monaghan Mushrooms' operations now include:

- Mushroom compost production
- Supply and erection of growing facilities to mushroom farms
- Mushroom growing

- Organising/controlling a franchised growing network
- Servicing the UK retail and food processing markets with quality fresh mushrooms, and
- Processing mushrooms in cans and jars for the European market.

FRESH MUSHROOMS

Monaghan Mushrooms has an impressive portfolio of customers for its fresh products, including all the major multiple retailers. It supplies, mostly on a non-exclusive basis, the "Big Five" chains in Britain: Sainsbury, Tesco, Safeway, ASDA and Somerfield, formerly Gateway (see Exhibit 2, UK Retail Mushroom Market, in the Appendices). The company offers an extensive range of fresh mushrooms, sized and graded to customer requirements. Monaghan Mushrooms has its own specialist transport fleet that collects the output from contracted growers, concentrating its operations at five depots. In addition to its operations at Tyholland, where indigenous production is aggregated, Monaghan Mushrooms has 30 large growing units, i.e. "houses", in the UK at Fenton Barnes, where the Irish group has an integrated centre combining production, collection, packaging, sales and distribution in Scotland, (see Table 2 in the Appendices). The Co. Monaghan plant remains the focus for "adding value", either through the "Fresh Division" or within processing operations, (e.g. canning), see below. In addition to the collection fleet, Monaghan Mushrooms operate a "mixed" delivery system (half company-owned and half contract hauliers) to their customers, the UK multiple retailers.

PROCESSING DIVISION

As well as being one of the leading suppliers of quality fresh products to the UK market, Monaghan Mushrooms is also a strong force in the food processing sector. In conjunction with its Fresh Division, the processing operation at Monaghan Mushrooms gives the company flexibility in the production and supply of quality mushrooms to many markets. Processing takes place within a "stainless steel environment" and, in line with its policy of continuously updating its plant, the company has recently installed modern profile-slicing and sterilisation equipment, undertaking laboratory testing and analysis throughout the process. The product range of whole and profile-sliced mushrooms is packed in a comprehensive range of sizes (cans and glass jars) for the retail, catering and food processing markets. Fresh sliced and semi-processed products are now supplied in large packs to food processors.

MAINTAINING STANDARDS/COMPETITIVENESS

New "satellite" growers are selected following interview by the management of the contracting "central organisation", i.e. Monaghan Mushrooms. When selected, they are supplied with a total mushroom growing package, incorporating a well defined code of practice for producing and harvesting the product. The growers are supported by professional advisory staff and quality assurance personnel who monitor and audit their performances. Incentive and award schemes motivate the growers to produce mushrooms to the required quality and hygiene standards. A stringent quality assurance programme has been adopted within the sector, with control systems operating throughout the chain — from the growers through to customer delivery. Only the highest quality mushrooms are delivered to meet the demands of "today's consumer, today"! Mechanical harvesting of the mushrooms is avoided in order to ensure a standard high quality end product.

The increasing popularity of mushrooms in today's fresh product market is the result of changing consumer attitudes towards healthier eating lifestyles. Monaghan's product range covers the whole spectrum of customer requirements and currently includes baby buttons, buttons, closed cups, open cups and flats in white and brown varieties, as well as canned products. Mushrooms are supplied to specification, in a comprehensive range of sizes in both metric and imperial weights. Monaghan Mushrooms operate a JIT ("just-in-time") system of deliveries, with "window slot" timing at multiple retail depots. The temperature-controlled transport fleets, cushioned with air suspension, collect the mushrooms from the growers and, after sorting, packing and cooling, the mushrooms are delivered daily to customers throughout the UK (see Exhibit 3 in the Appendices).

ADVANTAGES OF THE IRISH SYSTEM

In recent years the performance of the mushroom sector in competing successfully on export markets indicates that the Irish system has a number of advantages, including:

- The central composter, by specialisation, can supply a compost material of the highest quality
- The grower with a relatively small unit and personal incentive can give great attention to detail
- The system of production in plastic bags on one level with a large air to bed ratio facilitates production of very high quality mushrooms with reasonable capital outlay, and
- The central marketing system guarantees a continuity of supply of high quality product and access to major customers.

As indicated, above, one of the main benefits, undoubtedly, has been the fact that the central marketing system developed by enterprises such as Monaghan Mushrooms.

> Note: Monaghan Mushrooms is so oriented towards international marketing that it has refrained, consistently, from supplying the domestic, Irish market.

ATTEMPTING TO STAY AT THE FOREFRONT

Through attention to quality, customer service, investment in technology, and R&D, Monaghan Mushrooms has attempted to become a trend setter for the industry (see Exhibits 4 and 5 in the Appendices) through:

- Investing in technology and enhance the quality of its product/service to customers
- Promoting mushrooms as a health food, and

- Maintaining its leading position within the European mushroom sector through development, acquisitions and diversification.

A breakdown of Monaghan's projected sales is given in Table 3, while the latest data on European production are contained in Table 4 in the Appendices. Details of recent acquisitions and corporate development at Monaghan Mushrooms are contained in Exhibit 6 in the Appendices.

CO-ORDINATION/ORGANISATIONAL DEVELOPMENT

An umbrella body representing composting/marketing companies, growers, and associated firms, e.g. spawn suppliers, the Irish Mushroom Growers Association, IMGA, was established several years ago and includes most of the "major players" such as Monaghan Mushrooms, Tyholland, Co. Monaghan; Carbury Mushrooms, Co. Kildare; Connaught Mushrooms, Galway; Greenhill Compost, Carnagh, Kilogy, Co. Longford; Marley Compost, Crush, Carrickroe, Co. Monaghan; and Walsh Mushrooms, Wexford. In addition, regional groups representing individual mushroom growers have IMGA membership. The industry, through IMGA, has devised a voluntary levy scheme on the basis of IR£0.5 contribution per tonne of compost. Approximately 10 per cent of this levy is devoted to IMGA's administration and the remainder to funding R&D projects. Basic and applied research is carried out for the industry, on an on-going basis, by *Teagasc*, both through its horticultural division at Kinsealy Research Centre and through its food research centre in Dunsinea, Co. Dublin. There is, also, a Mushroom Research Group at the National Agricultural and Veterinary Biotechnology Centre, University College, Dublin.

In addition to the advisory services provided by the industry's major firms, short intensive courses, both for new mushroom growers and to assist the transfer of technology to existing farm enterprises, are organised under the aegis of Teagasc. *An Bord Glas* operates a National Auditing programme and in 1993 instituted its National Hygiene Awards for the mushroom industry. It recently announced incorporation of its Award scheme (organised on a regional basis) within the auditing programme.

IRISH MUSHROOMS: PERFORMANCE/PROSPECTIVE FUTURE

It has been acknowledged, generally, that the mushroom sector has been the main success story of Irish horticulture (see Table 5 in the Appendices). The sector doubled full-time jobs to 1,400 and increased part-time employment to 4,000 in the period 1988/1992. Its sales, the majority in the UK, have doubled to IR£54 million in the past seven years.[3]

A potential for controlled, market-led expansion in the mushroom industry, leading to additional employment of 3,000 (880 full-time and 2,200 part-time) is foreseen by Teagasc.[4] Significantly, the mushroom industry has been targeted as the main plank in a new five-year-plan,[5] presented to the government in June 1994 by *An Bord Glas* (literally "The Green Board" in the Irish language), the Horticultural Development Board. Brendan O'Donnell, chief executive, *An Bord Glas*, believes that:

> "the UK market provides the main opportunity — a study of the German market, the largest in Europe, has shown it is not commercially viable to export fresh horticultural products to it."

The state board has been given comparatively extensive powers and funding to develop and promote the Irish horticultural sector, with statutory powers to impose levies within the horticultural industry but, to date, it has preferred to encourage co-operative efforts in undertaking initiatives in training and R&D for the mushroom sector.

APPARENT DANGERS ON THE HORIZON

However, in spite of optimistic projections of future growth, several potentially serious threats to the Irish mushroom sector have arisen:

---

[3] Murphy, C. (1994): "Horticulture Plan Looks to UK Market", *Sunday Tribune*, 5 June 1994.

[4] "A Strategy for Horticultural Development", September 1994, *Teagasc*, Kinsealy.

[5] *"Mushroom News"* , vol. 2, no. 1, 2 and 3, March, June and October 1994, *An Bord Glas,* Dublin.

1. The first five months of 1992 had represented a period of relative exchange rate stability, with reserves rising and interest rate differentials *vis-à-vis* other Exchange Rate Mechanism, ERM, countries narrowing to historically low levels. Conditions began to deteriorate in June, however, when the prospect of steady progress towards Economic and Monetary Union (EMU) was questioned, following rejection of provisions of the Maastricht Treaty in the first Danish referendum on further integration of the EU.

   The following statement describes the ensuing events, from the Irish perspective:

   > "Pressures intensified in September, 1992 and remained for the rest of the year. Liquidity conditions deteriorated sharply and money market interest rates rose to unprecedented levels as the Central Bank utilised increases in its overnight support rate to defend the currency. Difficulties persisted in early 1993 and, eventually, the Irish pound's central rate was realigned within the ERM on 30 January 1993."[6]

   After an expensive defence of the Irish currency over five months, in the latter half of 1992 and the beginning of 1993,[7] the IR£ was devalued in line with sterling but, later, became one of the strongest currencies within the European Monetary System, EMS, "upper band" (see Exhibit 7 and Table 6 in the Appendices), raising fears of a prospective drastic decline in profit margins for Irish horticulture and the mushroom industry, in particular. Fluctuations in exchange rates, particularly pressures on the Irish "punt" *vis-à-vis* UK sterling, can pose major problems for the Irish mushroom industry, as occurred during the major upheaval on European financial markets in Autumn 1992. This instability on the money markets resulted in devaluation of most of the EU currencies, including UK sterling, to a more significant degree than initially occurred in the case of the IR punt. Consequently, it was widely reported

---

[6] Central Bank of Ireland Annual Report, 1992, (incorporating *Quarterly Bulletin*, Summer 1993), Dublin: Central Bank

[7] Leddin, A.J., "Unemployment and EMS Membeship", Labour Market Review, Winter 1992, FÁS, Training and Employment Authority, Dublin.

that many of the elements of the Irish economy, including the mushroom sector, suffered heavily in terms of export competitiveness.

2. Since the late 1950s the Irish government has been anxious to provide as many incentives as possible to encourage development of the industrial sector — in particular by attracting overseas firms to establish manufacturing facilities to serve European markets. Up to the 1980s a benign fiscal system designated that all profits on exports were tax-free. However, as a result of joining the European Community in 1973, the Irish government were forced to eliminate any discrimination in its tax policy in relation to firms selling on the domestic vs. export markets.

   Due to provisions for derogation from the European regulations, the Irish government had a lengthy period in which to develop an appropriate response strategy. Mushroom production was deemed to be "manufacturing" up to recently and thus qualified for the preferential rate of 10 per cent corporate tax which the Irish government had applied to the manufacturing sector of the economy. However, in 1993, following pressure from its own mushroom growers, the British government submitted a formal complaint to the European Commission concerning the Irish preferential rate, claiming "unfair competition" — since a standard rate of corporate tax, 27 per cent, was applied across the UK embracing all industries, the horticultural sector included. The Dublin government was forced by Brussels to declassify mushroom production as "manufacturing" and, under the Finance Bill 1994, imposed the standard 40 per cent corporation profit tax rate on mushroom producing companies, with composting companies retaining their 10 per cent tax status.

3. One can see some storm clouds gathering due to a claimed increase in production capacity in Holland. Mushrooms are among the most important horticultural crops in the Netherlands with 190,000 tonnes harvested in 1993. Exports of fresh mushrooms have grown to 50,000 tonnes, with the UK being the second largest customer of Dutch fresh mushrooms in 1993

— British sales representing 19 per cent, or 9,500 tonnes, of mushroom exports from the Netherlands.

4. In the UK, multiple supermarkets continue to predominate as the main channels for the household purchase of fresh produce. The multiples' share of the market is still growing, having control of in excess of 60 per cent of the retail market segment (in terms of volume). The major chains are continually competing aggressively with each other to increase their individual market shares. Currently, the multiple chains are involved in a "price war" — with fresh produce, including mushrooms, being a prime target. Loose mushrooms, which up to recently had achieved a selling price of £1.53/lb without seemingly having any negative adverse effect on consumption, are now being sold below this price level. On the other hand, the consumer can purchase more mushrooms at a reduced cost by choosing from the "valu-pack" ranges, e.g. 750 grams retailing at £1.59, or 1 lb packs retailing at £0.89, etc. It is known that Irish mushroom producers are attempting to gauge the likely effects of these developments on the sector and to develop appropriate strategies to guard their respective market shares.

5. In the medium to long term, availability of straw could prove to be a critical factor. Increased "setaside" provisions under the CAP (Common Agricultural Policy) programme released over 86,500 acres of land from cereal production in Ireland in 1994. When the effects of this EU measure are combined with the potentially increased demand for straw from the thriving Northern Ireland export market, there is the threat of a significant increase in the price of straw to Irish mushroom growers, who may be forced to import straw from the UK. On the other hand, there could be an increase in the indigenous supply of this critical raw material due to production of longer straw, as a result of EU prohibition of growth regulators under REPS (the Rural Environment Protection Scheme).

6. Ireland is probably the only country where mushrooms are entirely hand picked. The work is done mainly by women who work hours which suit their personal and domestic situations. The introduction of the new Workers' Protection Act by the

Irish government means that new rates of PRSI (Pay Related Social Insurance) now apply to casual workers. Some pickers are now saying they will discontinue because of the risk of losing Social Welfare benefits, since if, "at the margin", part-time earnings from mushroom picking are added to existing family income, they and their families may lose some entitlements. It is feared that the mushroom sector will find it difficult to survive without a plentiful supply of casual labour, and a strong case has been made for retention of the Farm Casual Scheme, allowing farmers to take on workers for purposes such as harvest cropping.

APPENDICES

TABLE 1: "ON-FARM" EMPLOYMENT, (COMBINED FULL-TIME AND PART-TIME), MONAGHAN MUSHROOMS, 1994

Location	Employers	No. of Employees
Republic of Ireland	Independent growers	945
Northern Ireland	"Kernans" ("MM") subsidiary	135
Scotland	"Monaghan Mushrooms" ("MM") Fenton Barnes, Edinburgh	65*
Total		1,145

* Mostly full-time, (contract employees of Monaghan Mushrooms).

Note: A member of Monaghan Mushrooms estimates that "on-farm" employment can be apportioned 15 per cent full-time and 85 per cent part-time, approximately.

TABLE 2: MONAGHAN MUSHROOMS DEPOTS/GROWERS ("HOUSES")

	Depot	*No. of Growers*	*("Houses")*
1	Tyholland, Co Monaghan	132	(590)
2	Glenveagh, Co Donegal	29	(118)
3	Foxfield, Kilnaleck, Co Cavan	49	(218)
4	Benburb, Co Tyrone, N Ireland	38	(166)
5	Fenton Barnes, Scotland — all large "houses"	3	(30)
	Total	275	(1,122)

EXHIBIT 1: MONAGHAN MUSHROOMS ORGANISATION CHART

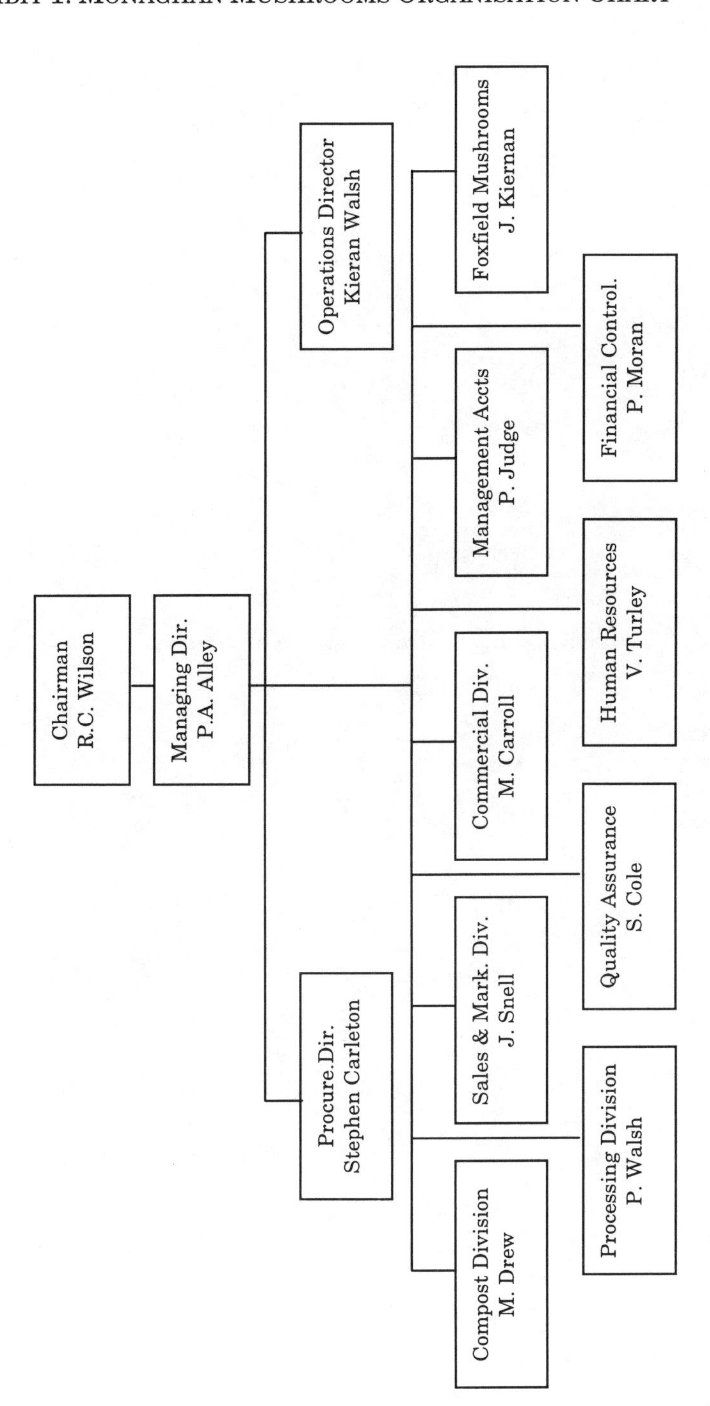

EXHIBIT 2: MONAGHAN MUSHROOMS: PRODUCTION AND DISTRIBUTION

EXHIBIT 3: UK RETAIL MUSHROOM MARKET, AUGUST 1994

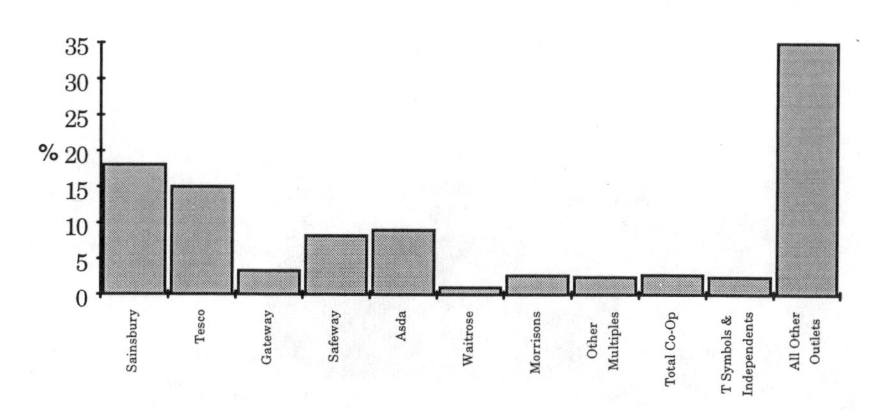

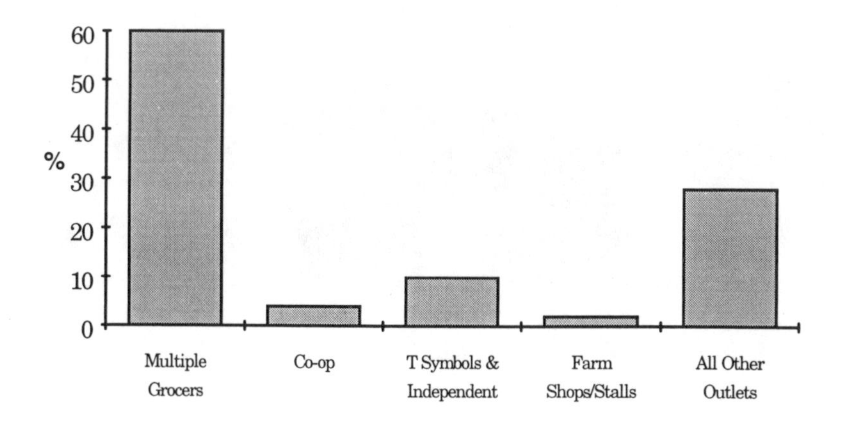

EXHIBIT 3: UK RETAIL MUSHROOM MARKET, AUGUST 1994 (CONTINUED)

Type Shares of Total Mushrooms Based on Volume (000 lb)

Total Market 16,704

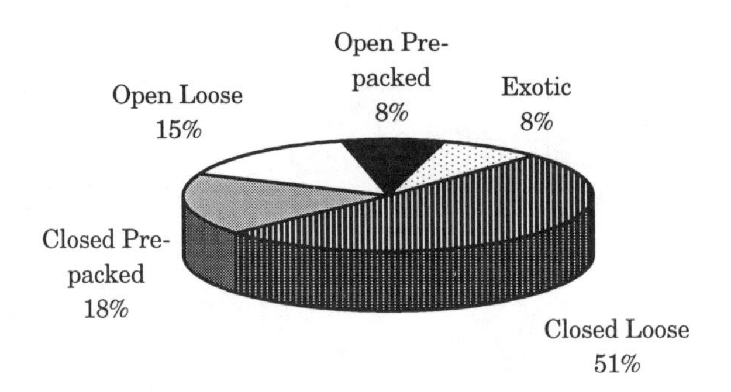

Type Shares of Defined Salad Vegetables Based on Expenditure (£000)

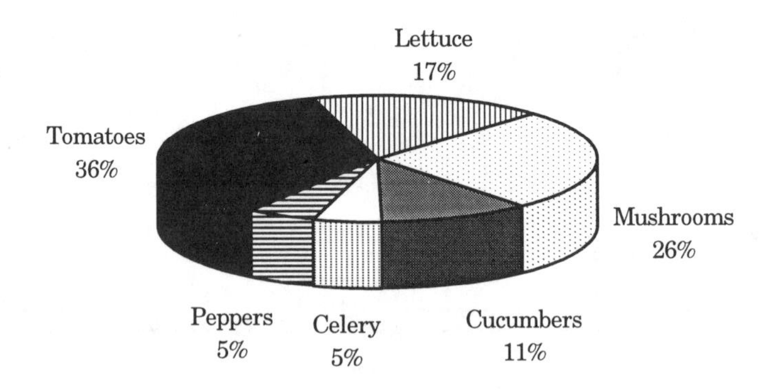

Source: "Mushroom News", published by An Bord Glas, October 1994, vol.2, no.3, pp 1-3.

Exhibit 4: Kabeyun Ltd: Compost Manufacture

Kabeyun Ltd., a wholly owned subsidiary of Pleroma, the holding company of the Monaghan Mushrooms group, is the largest producer of mushroom compost in Britain or Ireland. Using advanced technology the company produces quality compost needed to yield firm white mushrooms with high dry matter content. As all the inputs of mushroom compost are natural materials, mainly straw and animal manure, there are consequent variations in their nutrient properties. The company imposes stringent monitoring of raw materials to ensure that the production processes give a consistent formula.

The Kabeyun enterprise strives to achieve consistency, through providing a wide range of expertise and other back-up resources, such as the following:

- Sophisticated blending equipment which mixes the raw materials in their correct proportions
- Computerised environmental control throughout the sterilisation process
- Laboratory analysis of raw materials and finished product
- Special facilities for filling and sealing the compost for the bag growing system, and
- An efficient fleet of distribution vehicles equipped with forklift trucks giving prompt delivery of the bagged compost to the growing units with minimum exposure to the elements.

The group has compost making facilities at four locations, including Scotland, and it has indicated that one of its prime missions is to be at the forefront of development in compost manufacture.

Exhibit 5: Clonkeen Mushroom Developments Ltd: Mushroom Technology and Horticultural Equipment

The Pleroma group also owns Clonkeen Mushroom Developments Ltd. Founded to service the expanding mushroom industry with growing units, the company's product range has expanded significantly in recent years. The firm is now a major supplier of growing tunnels, control technology and ancillary supplies to the mushroom and horticultural sectors in Ireland. The company's R&D team is available to assist in the design and development of custom designed facilities.

The current product range offered by Clonkeen Mushroom Developments includes the following facilities and equipment:

- Growing tunnels constructed from quality heavy wall (2mm) steel tubing which has been hot dipped galvanised for lasting protection against corrosion. Units are insulated with 120mm fibre glass between two 1,000-gram polythene covers.
- Twin fan ventilation systems designed to give accurate and fully automatic environmental control in the growing tunnels.
- Cooling systems with specially designed 6 row cooling coil.
- Control equipment giving temperature and humidity readings on a digital display unit.
- CO_2 meters complete with water separator, piping and filters, and
- Production supplies — thermometers, watering and harvesting equipment.

EXHIBIT 6: PROFILE/RONNIE WILSON

In October 1994, Monaghan Mushrooms purchased Britain's second largest mushroom producer, Middlebrook Farms, for an undisclosed sum. The deal should increase Monaghan Mushroom's annual turnover, currently estimated at £50 million, by about 40 per cent, and its successful completion has transformed Ronnie Wilson into one of the major players in the £400 million British and Irish mushroom market. Most Irish companies would have made quite a hullabaloo about such a deal, but that is not Mr Wilson's style. The negotiations and sale of Middlebrook, which has its headquarters at Avon, south of Bristol, were completed in secret and when news of the deal broke Mr Wilson declined to comment. Some Irish agriculture sources were surprised by the Middlebrook deal as the UK company is a direct employer, and operates large commercial farms. It would appear to be exactly the sort of operation that Mr Wilson and Monaghan out-manoeuvred in the 1980s.

In stereotypical, Ulsterman fashion Ronnie Wilson says very little and generally keeps himself to himself. He is reputed to be a straight talker and a shrewd but tough negotiator. According to colleagues, he is a workaholic who adopts a hands-on approach to everything. One said that his only problem may be delegating responsibility, and letting go sufficiently to allow himself time to explore other directions. Until quite recently the soft spoken Mr Wilson met his growers on a regular basis, but he has now handed over the day-to-day running of the mushroom business to his management team. While the humble mushroom has made him a great deal of money, the former school teacher has a lifestyle that belies his wealth. Ronnie Wilson is rarely interviewed, even more rarely photographed and could conceivably be termed Ireland's most reclusive businessman. He still lives in Tyholland, Co. Monaghan with the company's compost and processing facilities within sight of his front door.

During its 15 years in business the turnover and profits of Monaghan Mushrooms have never been revealed. With annual sales of £50 million, market analysts believe that the company generates profits of about £3 million a year. The actual ownership of Pleroma, the holding company which owns Monaghan and Middlebrook is also a matter of some conjecture. It is known that Mr Wilson, who is its chief executive, holds a majority stake in the company while a substantial minority stake, thought to be about 30 per cent, is held by Mercury Asset Management, the investment arm of the British merchant bank S.G. Warburg. The Scottish businessman Mr Joe Barber, who is the chairman of Pleroma, is also believed to have a stake in the company.

In the early 1990s Monaghan bought competitors Foxfield of Cavan and Kernans of Armagh which had a combined turnover of £21 million. Ronnie Wilson entered the pig processing market in February 1994 with the purchase of the troubled Uniport group and he now spends most of his time at its headquarters in Cookstown, Co Tyrone. Mr Wilson has a strategic vision to expand Pleroma into a broad based food company, and he is reported to be interested in purchasing the former Tunney meats plant in Clones. He was also part of a consortium that made a failed bid for Leckpatrick Dairies which was bought by Golden Vale.

Source: Adaptation of O'Kane, Paul, "Mushrooming Millions", Business This Week, *The Irish Times*, 14 October 1994

EXHIBIT 7: IR£'S PERFORMANCE ON FINANCIAL MARKETS, 1992-93

EMS stability was dramatically shaken in September 1992 when sterling and the lira left the Exchange Rate Mechanism (ERM) and, along with the Spanish peseta, were devalued. It is estimated that well over a billion pounds left Irish financial markets in a few days. The Central Bank's external reserves fell nearly £2 billion, from £3.05 billion at the end of August to £1.07 billion at the end of September.

There were four distinct phases in the management of the Irish pound exchange rate during 1992 and the early part of 1993. The first, from January to May, was a period of relative exchange rate stability. During the second phase, from June to mid-September, tensions in the European Monetary System (EMS) resulted in sizeable negative foreign exchange interventions and higher interest rates in support of the Irish currency. The third phase was from mid-September to January 1993, during which time there was intermittent severe pressure on the Irish pound. Over this period, the external reserves were depleted, the EMS support system was extensively utilised and domestic liquidity conditions tightened significantly as pressures on the currency culminated in a realignment of the Irish pound within the ERM on 30 January 1993. The final phase — February to April 1993 — was marked by a significant improvement in sentiment in the foreign exchange and money markets. Before the end of March, interest rates were reduced below pre-crisis levels, outstanding debts for market support were repaid and the external reserves were rebuilt.

Sterling had always been the Achilles' heel of Ireland's EMS policy. The view of foreign investors was that the Irish pound was susceptible to devaluation during periods of sterling weakness — the devaluation of the IR£ in 1983 and 1986 provided ample justification. Hence, when sterling devalued in September 1992, foreign investors withdrew their funds from Ireland in order to avoid incurring a capital loss. However, contrary to the earlier episodes, the Central Bank decided in September, 1992 not to devalue but, instead, to raise interest rates to defend the exchange rate.

Since a devaluation in 1986, the Irish government had pursued a policy of fixing the IR£ in the EMS band in order to keep interest rates and inflation close to the German levels. The government was intent on sticking to this policy despite the sterling depreciation. There was a danger, of course, that the loss of competitiveness associated with the sterling devaluation would reduce Irish exports and increase imports.

In order to compensate for this, the government introduced a "market development fund" which paid IR£50 per job per week to firms affected by the devaluation of sterling. This fund was intended to be only a temporary measure as it was expected that sterling would appreciate in the near future and the trading difficulties facing Irish firms would disappear. In the event, the UK£ did not appreciate within the expected time span, leading to the forecast by one commentator that the "market development fund" was destined to "prove unworkable and effective").[6]

TABLE 3: PROJECTED SALES, MONAGHAN MUSHROOMS 1994

Fresh Division	IR£36.5 million
Processed Products	IR £6.5 million
Total	IR£43.0 million

TABLE 4: EU MUSHROOM PRODUCTION 1992

Country	*Tonnes (000s)*
France	220
Netherlands	190
UK	118
Italy	115
Germany	60
Ireland	41
Belgium	31 (*)
Denmark	N/A.
Spain	N/A.
Luxembourg	N/A.
Portugal	N/A.
Greece	N/A.
Total	780 (**)

(*) = 1991 figure; (**) = Estimated global production for the EU.

Source: "Mushroom News", Vol. 1, No. 3, December 1993: Vol. 2, No. 1, March, 1994, *An Bord Glas,* Dublin.

TABLE 5: IRELAND MUSHROOM PRODUCTION 1980-93, (000 TONNES)

Year	*"Fresh" Home Market*	*"Fresh" UK Exports*	*"Processed" Exports*	*Total Production*
1980	1.8	5.0		6.8
1981	1.7	5.4	0.6	7.7
1982	2.4	5.2	1.8	9.4
1983	3.2	5.4	2.5	11.1
1984	4.6	6.0	3.3	13.9
1985	4.8	9.4	4.1	18.3
1986	6.2	8.5	3.4	18.1
1987	6.2	12.1	2.7	21.0
1988	7.0	13.1	2.2	22.4
1989	9.1	18.0	3.5	30.6
1990	7.6	26.2	3.0	36.8
1991	7.7	27.0	4.5	39.2
1992	8.7	29.1	3.2	41.0
1993	9.5	32.5	2.0	44.0

Source: "Mushroom News", Vol. 2, No. 1, March 1994, 4. *An Bord Glas,* Dublin.

Note: While the average annual rate of growth of production within the EU was 5.5 per cent (compound), Irish producers achieved an average of 16.3 per cent per annum over this period.

TABLE 6: EXCHANGE RATES IN DUBLIN MARKET, 1992/1994: PERIOD AVERAGES

	v. UK£		v. UK£	v. D.Mk	ECU	Effective Index*
Jan '92	0.9323					
Feb '92	0.9275					
Mar '92	0.9312	Qtr 1, 1992	0.9304	2.6662	1.3053	67.98
Apr '92	0.9209					
May '92	0.9101					
Jun '92	0.9158	Qrt 2, 1992	0.9155	2.6692	1.3013	67.63
Jul '92	0.9320					
Aug '92	0.9434					
Sept '92	0.9861	Qrt 3, 1992	0.9538	2.6530	1.3087	69.81
Oct '92	1.0705					
Nov '92	1.0892					
Dec '92	1.0753	Qrt 4,1992	1.0784	2.6363	1.3426	72.50
Jan '93	1.0673					
Feb '93	0.9622	(**)				
Mar '93	0.9677	Qtr 1, 1993	1.0353	2.4995	1.2834	68.85
Apr '93	0.9882					
May '93	0.9800					
Jun '93	0.9772	Qtr 2, 1993	0.9817	2.4386	1.2486	66.40
Jul '93	0.9425					
Aug '93	0.9324					
Sep '93	0.9421	Qtr 3, 1993	0.9391	2.3676	1.2283	64.00
Oct '93	0.9542					
Nov '93	0.9491					
Dec '93	0.9516	Qtr 4, 1993	0.9516	2.3881	1.2442	64.72
Jan '94	0.9597					
Feb '94	0.9603					
Mar '94	0.9619	Qrt 1, 1994	0.9607	2.4625	1.2706	65.50

(*) Trade weighted exchange rate index for the IR£ (base 1971 = 100)

(**) Realignment of the EMS (European Monetary System) occurred on 30 January 1993, resulting in an effective 10 per cent devaluation of the IR£.

7

ROCKERS FOR WALKERS BY CHEROKEE FROM JAMES BOYLAN AND SON LTD.: A CASE STUDY IN A NEW PRODUCT LAUNCH[1]

Gerry Mortimer

THE COMPANY

In 1995, James Boylan and Son Ltd. was celebrating its fiftieth year of trading, though its origins dated back further. It was still mostly owned by the Boylan family who had controlled it since its inception. The company was based in the tiny and now largely deserted village of Mullan close to Emyvale in Co. Monaghan in the Irish Republic. It was located about 400 metres from the border with Northern Ireland, though the road was impassable to vehicular traffic. The bridge, which traversed the river that marked the border, had been blown up some 20 years previously by the British Army at the height of what were known as "the troubles". As a result there was a detour of some 10 miles to cross the border.

The name Mullan derives from the Irish word *muileann* which means "mill". There had been a flax mill at that location dating back to the early 19th century. Eventually the mill had closed and was replaced by a shoe manufacturing plant on the same site. Apart from the mill, the village consists of about 30 cottages which had very limited facilities and a few modern houses. The cottages were owned by the company and were in poor repair though there was a proposal being considered to renovate them in association with the local community. There was a long tradition

---

[1] This case was developed as a basis for class discussion rather than to illustrate either effective or ineffective handling of an administrative situation. It is dedicated to the memory of James Boylan, son of Jim and grandson of the founder of the company, whose death at a tragically early age was an immense loss to his family and family business.

of footwear manufacture in the adjacent counties of Monaghan and Louth, though James Boylan and Son Ltd (JBS) was one of the few to survive major changes in the 1960s and 1970s.

Various branches of the family had established manufacturing, wholesaling, importing and retail operations in various parts of the country. The James Boylan branch of the family had concentrated on manufacturing and wholesaling of footwear. In particular, Boylan boots were a byword in rural Ireland for strength and durability. That the Boylan boot was no longer manufactured, due to intense competition from imports, particularly from Eastern Europe, is a reflection of changed times in the footwear market.

James Boylan's son, Jim, joined the company in the early 1960s during which period it was rationalised into separate manufacturing and wholesale operations based in Monaghan and Dublin respectively. Jim first managed the manufacturing operation and subsequently, on his father's retirement, took control of the wholesale operation. He brought professional footwear management into the Monaghan operation. Eventually in the early 1980s the wholesale operation in Dublin was transferred to Monaghan to merge with the manufacturing business. Jim took the opportunity, thus presented, to reduce his day-to-day involvement with the business and turned the wholesale company into a successful property holding company while pursuing academic and consultancy interests. He remained as chairman of JBS though on a largely non-executive basis. Although the company shrank in size, particularly in manufacturing, it continued to trade satisfactorily, though it did experience some poor years in the difficult trading conditions of the mid-1980s.

In response to changing market conditions the product ranges produced and imported by the company evolved. In manufacturing it mainly focused on work boots, major contracts for groups such as army and prison services and mid-price range mens and boys shoes. Imports depended largely on items which were in fashion, though JBS was an agent for Dr Martens footwear. It shared this with three other agents though rationalisation was expected in these arrangements in 1995. Dr Martens products were highly successful and JBS was on allocation from the manufacturers through the early 1990s. JBS had, however, increased its allocation on several occasions. Dr Martens products represented a substantial part of JBS distribution and the company had been keen to develop other lines.

In 1990, Jim's son James joined the company. He had qualified as an engineer and had worked for some years in the oil industry in the UK. Jim had long been keen to see the torch pass to the next generation and was delighted when James became involved. James' influence on the company quickly became significant. He had little interest in manufacturing and primarily focused on the distribution end of the business. He sought new brands to represent, with some success. He formalised the division between manufacturing and distribution. Each part of the business was now treated as a separate entity with separate accounts and was obliged to stand alone. There was still some overlap between the two divisions as consumer products, which were manufactured in-house by JBS, were marketed by the distribution division. The manufacturing division also refocused its efforts and identified a significant opportunity in industrial footwear. New health and safety regulations made this a growth market. By marketing direct to end-users such as major industrial concerns, local authorities and other public services, JBS share of this sector began to grow rapidly. The sector was largely dominated by one major Irish manufacturer and a number of importer/distributors who also tended to deal in other safety equipment. Industrial or safety footwear was characterised by attributes such as steel toes, steel mid-soles, non-skid, chemical-resistant and anti-static features. John Bond, who managed the manufacturing division, and his staff had recognised a demand for good quality, competitively priced, Irish made, safety footwear. By focusing on major buyers, JBS had quadrupled its market share in four years and held an estimated 15 per cent in 1995. It was confident of some further growth. This, allied to its contract business for army and prison services, now constituted the major portions of the manufacturing division's turnover. In fact, by the end of 1994 the manufacturing division had virtually ceased to produce for the distribution division. Although they shared administration and premises costs, the split was now complete. After a few lean years the division had, by now, returned to modest profits.

JBS DISTRIBUTION

In the meantime James Boylan had set out to develop the distribution business. He cut costs and improved margins, improving profitability considerably as a result. He also sought to develop new brands, principally through importing. Most successful brands, such as Nike and Caterpillar, were either distributed by the brand owners or an established agent. He had some successes, notably with Kangaroos though lack of international brand support had eventually caused Kangaroos' sales to fall after encouraging sales in the early 1990s. This illustrated a common problem in branding of footwear in Ireland. The market was small and significant brand support was difficult to justify unless there was also some international support, or a very high market share, or both. As an example, JBS had taken on an agency for a Spanish trainer range called Roobins. This was competitively priced and reasonably distinctive, but did not justify marketing support and had eventually been discontinued.

Tragically, in 1992 James became ill, and though he returned briefly to work the following year he suffered a relapse and died early in 1994 at the age of 30. As chairman, Jim was obliged to increase his involvement temporarily. Rather than impose a new structure on the division, Jim allowed a situation to evolve where the division was managed jointly by Liam Stirrat, the senior sales representative, Noel McGuirke, who was responsible for purchasing and warehousing, and Ann Flannery, who managed the administration function.

The policies developed by James were continued. The division was profitable. The major selling brands continued to be Dr Martens and a range of Boylan brands which were known within the company as the JayBees range. As an individual brand, JayBees was mostly used on boys' shoes which were described as "back to school" in Autumn or "confirmation" in Spring. There were also a range of sub-brands which were generally developed in response to changing market conditions. Some examples were as follows:

> **Hymacs:** This was a range of boots targeted at late teens/early twenties of both sexes. It was based on the highly successful Caterpillar brand which had enjoyed considerable success in world shoe markets in 1993 and 1994.

Emyvale: This was a range of chunky casual shoes targeted at adult males.

Heros: These were ranges of boots and shoes with raised soles and heels targeted at the teenage market.

Many of these brands also carried the James Boylan or JayBees brand.

Management in JBS accepted that the brands were weak and mostly developed as a reaction to market changes. It was, however, difficult to put serious support behind a particular brand which might not survive for more than a season. Market trends will be discussed in the following section. In total, JBS had an estimated 2 per cent market share divided roughly equally between safety/contract and consumer.

During 1994 a series of decisions were made by JBS which were designed to improve marketing of their own brands:

- New promotional literature was introduced, though this was principally aimed at industrial customers and owners of brands being targeted by JBS for possible distribution arrangements.

- The James Boylan brand was reformulated and was gradually being introduced to all promotional material such as literature, stationery, socks (inside shoes), boxes, bags and point of sale material. Other brands would be phased out or would become subsidiary to the James Boylan brand.

- A monthly newsletter was developed which was dispatched with statements to the company's 500 retailer customers situated throughout Ireland. This informed retailers of developments within the company, special offers, new ranges and general information about the footwear industry.

- A tele-sales operation was formally established in Mullan. This was used by both divisions and had improved contacts with customers between visits by sales representatives.

However, most marketing effort was expended on a personal selling operation. The safety/contract division had two sales representatives. The senior of these also handled head office marketing functions such as range development, literature and contract negotiation. The manager of the division was also involved in selling to the top 10 accounts out of a customer base approaching 200. At the end of 1994 the division was also in the process of recruiting a sales representative for Northern Ireland, which had been targeted following a market research project partly sponsored by Acumen, a North/South initiative which itself was sponsored by a number of development agencies and the International Fund for Ireland.

The distribution division also had two full-time sales representatives together with two agents who sold other footwear lines. These latter operated on a commission basis with a defined territory and range to sell. One covered Northern Ireland but was not, in 1994, generating significant sales. The sales representatives serviced customers on a monthly or six week cycle. Their functions were to take orders, introduce ranges, handle complaints and returns, merchandise and generally keep in touch with market trends.

In total, JBS distribution had some 500 retail accounts throughout Ireland. This was heavily skewed away from the Dublin area where the presence was modest. Various reasons were advanced for this. JBS had traditionally had a strong presence in rural areas from its "Boylan Boots" days. The standard small town owner-managed retailer still held sway outside major cities. However, within the cities, department stores, UK-based chains and specialist shops offering a narrow, focused range were increasing share. JBS did not have a major presence with any of these groupings though efforts were being made to redress this.

Outside the Dublin area, JBS serviced over 80 per cent of all outlets in the Irish Republic, though it was rarely one of the biggest suppliers to any retailer. This reflected the disparate nature of the market and the lack of leading brands under JBS sole control. Nevertheless, this business continued to be profitable for JBS. In total, JBS employed some 60 staff.

THE IRISH FOOTWEAR MARKET

Reliable information on the Irish footwear market was difficult to obtain. However, an EIU report had estimated that the market at ex-factory or import level was worth IR£140 million (about the same in £Stg) in 1991. This was estimated to represent some 18 million pairs or just under 6 pairs per head of population of 3.5 million. The same report also indicated an import penetration of 103 per cent. Given that there were some level of domestic manufacture and some exports (though not by JBS), this suggested that there was a significant level of re-exporting taking place. In any event, the figures were of limited value. They indicated an average price of about £8 per pair which masked the inclusion of everything from flip-flops to Gucchi.

However, some general trends could be established:

- Demand for footwear was static. There was, however, some growth in certain areas such as the aforementioned safety footwear.

- There were also annual patterns of demand with sales peaking in the final quarter. In Ireland, weather patterns also appeared to have an effect on sales. In particular, unseasonal weather had an adverse effect on sales. For example, bad weather in May and June affected sales of summer ranges. Likewise, good weather in late Autumn/early Winter also tended to reduce demand. In both cases consumers delayed purchase decisions for a particular season and then were less likely to proceed with a purchase designed for a shorter season.

- Imports into the EU had doubled between 1985 and 1990 and were continuing to increase. By 1990 imports represented over 75 per cent of the market in pairage though significantly less than that in value. The growth from low-cost producers was even more significant with countries such as China, Indonesia and Thailand showing increases of up to 7-fold in that period. A pattern was emerging whereby the brand was being separated from its production. Many of the major owners of brands did not, in fact, manufacture at all. Rather they sub-contracted out to producers in low-cost countries. High quality, expensive footwear continued to be manufactured in Europe and, indeed, presented some export opportunities.

Local manufacturers had some advantages such as greater flexibility and better quality control. However, the trends were all in the opposite direction and JBS recognised that it might not be manufacturing in 10 years time. Already it was sourcing much of its product in the UK including products which it carried under its own brands.

- The market was very fashion conscious. This was particularly true of the higher ticket items. While there were classic or standard designs, they were becoming fewer with markets such as children and safety footwear becoming more fashion conscious. In addition, fashion trends were diffusing much more rapidly than before. JBS management had often commented that major fashion developments had taken some months to reach Dublin from major centres such as London or Paris, and then further months to reach other parts of Ireland. Given that JBS strength lay in the latter market, this had frequently allowed for time to develop, test and sell a range and to obtain a significant level of repeat orders. Often, it was on repeat orders that the profit was made as development costs had been absorbed. This had all changed and the diffusion was now almost instantaneous, putting additional pressure on small manufacturers such as JBS. The company watched market trends closely and attended all major footwear fairs. This was a vital part of any footwear manufacturer's operation. It was very easy to be left with unsaleable stock when a trend moved on.

- Figures for market share were difficult to establish. However, patterns of competition at manufacturer/distribution level could be ascertained. Here two significant trends were apparent. Own brand drapery stores, principally Dunnes Stores, had become a major player. Dunnes sourced their own footwear, mostly in low-cost countries. Their products were positioned as low price/good value. Perhaps because of this, they had significant image problems, particularly in the teen and sub-teen markets which were highly brand conscious. A second major development was the growth in retail chains from the UK such as Clarks and Saxone. They imported and, in most cases, branded their own goods, though some established brands, such as Dr Martens, were carried by such chains. Parallel importing of ranges, for which there were established agents in Ireland, also appeared to be common among such outlets. A third significant trend was in the growth of specialist retailers who focused on a particular niche. Marathon, Lifestyle, Zerep and Great Outdoors were examples of this trend. They tended to purchase established brands from existing agents. Most of these trends were more noticeable in large urban areas such as Dublin and Cork.

In addition to these there were perhaps 15-20 active distributors. In a few cases, they represented only one product such as one of the large trainer brands. In others, like JBS, they had developed from traditional wholesale or manufacturing operations. Examples were Stafford Mitchell and Drummies. The latter also operated at retail level owning a number of outlets specialising in Ecco shoes for which they were the distributors.

There were also a number of manufacturers with operations in Ireland. Of these, the largest was Dubarry whose market share would still have been in low single figures, though they also exported. They were probably the only footwear manufacturer in Ireland employing more than 100 staff. This contrasted with the boom periods when Clarks and Woodingtons employed up to 2,500 each. Other manufacturers were Whelans, Padmore and Barnes and Blackthorn. All held a small market share.

At retail level the trends mentioned above were having an impact. In particular, the growth of Dunnes Stores, specialist outlets and UK-based chains were all having an effect on the market. Nevertheless, the small town owner-managed retailer continued to survive, though there was some evidence that greater mobility among shoppers was increasing the share of outlets in larger regional centres at the expense of small town outlets. The shoe trade at retail level was not seen as glamorous or attractive. As a result, succession in small outlets was a problem and they frequently closed when the owner retired. Many smaller retailers were not serviced at all by major brands. Nike, for example, were marketed direct from the UK and could only justify dealing with larger outlets, usually in main centres of population. The smaller outlets were frequently easier to access and the relationship between sales representatives and clients were close. It could be difficult to reproduce that type of relationship in an urban operation which was likely to be staffed by sales assistants and a manager who did not have buying authority. In Dublin, many of the largest retail outlets were based in department stores such as Arnotts, Brown Thomas and Clerys. In general, the trade was changing and not many of the changes were likely to be of benefit to JBS. The directors fully recognised this and had also been adopting a policy which would see them develop towards becoming managers of successful brands.

With regard to price, the price point at retail level was regarded as crucial. Many consumers entered a shop with, apparently, a price range in mind. This, of course, had implications for assessing the importance of the role of the shop assistant in influencing the purchase. It was common for retailers to double the VAT exclusive price of a product which they had purchased. Thus, a pair of shoes purchased by the retailer for £20 plus VAT might sell out at £39.99 inclusive of VAT. No VAT was charged on children's shoes. Dunnes Stores were assumed to work to smaller margins as did UK-based chains. However, in the latter case this may have been a transfer pricing exercise to minimise profit, and thus corporation tax, in Ireland.

THE OPPORTUNITY

In pursuance of the JBS strategy of developing new brands and monitoring market trends, Liam Stiratt and Noel McGuirke visited a major US shoe fair in Las Vegas in August 1994. Among the contacts made were with a California-based company called Cherokee. They were specialists in footwear targeted at older casual users and those who walked extensively. Their ranges included leather sandals, hiking and climbing boots and trainers which were rather understated. Noel and Liam recognised that market conditions in the US and Europe were different, but they were taken with a range of which Cherokee claimed to have sold 450,000 pairs in less than 18 months. The shoes were similar to trainers or light walking shoes. They had plain leather uppers and rubber soles. They were available in a limited range of colours such as sand, white, grey and black. What intrigued Noel and Liam was the design of the sole. What could only be described as a bump on the sole at the arch of the foot meant that if the shoe was placed on a flat surface, it rocked on the "bump" so that either the toe and the "bump" or the heel and the "bump" were resting on the surface at the same time. The presence of the "bump" meant that the heel and toe could not make contact with the ground at the same time. In walking, apparently, the foot was thrown forward by the "bump" which from front to back represented a small segment of a circle just over an inch in length. The rocking motion, thus created, had led to the shoes being branded as Rockers. The sole was patented. Hence, the unwieldy title of this case study for which the author apologises.

When Liam and Noel returned to Ireland, they reported back to the management group on the contacts made. By now Jim's younger son, Grattan, had returned from working abroad and had taken up a marketing position with JBS, particularly focusing on new products.

A range of samples arrived from Cherokee some weeks later. By now it was evident that any launch of the product would not take place until the Spring of 1995. This offered time to consider a strategy in detail. The management group considered the project in some detail and came to the following preliminary conclusions:

- The shoes were well manufactured, though there were some inconsistencies in styles and sizes. This apparently arose as some were manufactured in Indonesia and some in Thailand. In particular, they did not correspond to the UK sizes indicated on the shoes. There was, in any event, a difference of 1.5 sizes between US and UK sizes but there was a further discrepancy of between 1 and 1.5 sizes from what would be expected. This would not be a major problem if retailers were properly briefed, though it was a nuisance. For example, it was difficult to find feet on which to try out the small number of samples sent!

- The shoes were available in narrow, standard and broad fittings. However, the group quickly came to the conclusion that

Irish feet were such that only broad, and possibly standard, fittings were of any relevance.

- The shoes were targeted exclusively at women. It became clear that the market would be mature women possibly from age 30 up. When one of the young clerical assistants in JBS tried on a pair she was asked for her comments. She threw the group into a slough of despondency by describing them as "awful". On being asked to further expand on this she agreed that they were "really comfortable but I wouldn't be seen dead in them". Samples shown to older women generated much greater enthusiasm. The likely price point of £40 or £45, depending on style, was also highly acceptable. It was proposed to develop a focus group which would be invited to try the shoes and report back on their views. Unfortunately, there were not enough suitable samples available for this purpose and it had to be abandoned. In fact obtaining samples presented many unforeseen problems. Cherokee had apparently never previously dealt in Europe though their turnover ran to tens of millions of dollars. They appeared unsure of how to proceed when JBS enquired about the possibility of exclusive distribution for Ireland.

- Promotional material supplied with the products was basic and of limited value. It appeared that advertising was confined to a specialist magazine called *The Walker* which appeared to circulate by subscription to walking enthusiasts. No such equivalent existed in Ireland. Other material consisted of bags, display boards and tee shirts.

- The 45-day walk test, which was promoted in the advertising, quickly became a major issue in the JBS group. This was an arrangement whereby any customer not satisfied with the product could return the shoes and obtain a refund, up to 45 days after purchase, with no questions asked. Given that the product was, at first glance, rather radical, this seemed to some to be an excellent idea. However, JBS would have to fund such a scheme as Cherokee would only refund JBS for defective goods. Part of the management group vehemently opposed such a suggestion on two grounds. In the first place, they claimed that Irish consumers would take advantage of such an opportunity and that JBS would be swamped with returns which would make the project uneconomic. Secondly, they argued that retailers would be very unenthusiastic about such a scheme. Cherokee's experience had been of minimal returns.

- Though not seeing the project as an outstanding opportunity, the management group decided to proceed with further analysis while negotiating an agreement with Cherokee. A small sub-group was set up to plan and manage a launch.

THE ISSUES

Turnover
It was agreed that a target of 5,000 pairs in a full year would have to be achieved to make the project worthwhile. At normal margins this would produce a turnover of £100,000. Sales representatives were confident that this could be achieved.

Positioning
Following the Cherokee positioning strategy might limit the market. On the other hand, a higher price might be obtainable for a specialist product. However, it should be recalled that each £1 added to the trade price would be doubled at the retail level. If the positioning was to be broadened out to a wider group than those who considered themselves to be active walkers, sales would be expect to be higher but would the product deliver the required benefit to a broader group? Comfort in walking was the main attribute of the product together with its sole and the plain understated styling.

Branding
A glance at the title of the case study indicates the dilemma here. Both Rockers and Cherokee are featured on the shoes, though not on a consistent basis. "Rockers" was on the side of some of the range but not on others. Both names featured in the sock and on the sole though neither were visible when worn. Neither brand

name was known in Ireland or in Europe though both words would be recognisable in other contexts.

Price

Price would depend on positioning. At standard mark-ups and based on a dollar value of $1.50 to IR£1.00, sale prices of between £20 and £22, both plus VAT, delivered to retailers would be satisfactory. However, they would not provide significant resources for promotion, unless sales greatly exceeded expectations of 5,000 pairs in the first year.

Distribution

This was an issue of major concern. The marketing group recognised that it would probably be unrealistic to sell to all retailers currently being serviced. Based on projections this would provide an average annual sale of 10 pairs and would hardly justify effort on the retailers' part. Neither would it convey a suitable image for a product which was intended to give an upmarket and relatively sophisticated image. In general, the project also offered an opportunity to target retailers with which JBS did not have a relationship, but would they be interested? If not, what might make them interested?

Promotion

Major decisions obviously also had to be made in this area. The group recognised that the projections indicated a limited budget for a product launch. Company management were willing to commit £10,000 to the project but would want to be thoroughly convinced of its value before committing more resources over and above this. Given the paucity of the promotional material available from the USA, the group would have to start from scratch in putting together a promotional plan. JBS had not tended to use advertising extensively in recent years but were well aware of the published rates. An example of the promotional material is given in Appendix 1. The following table illustrates the key features of rates in selected journals.

Magazine	*Circulation*	*Cost Per Page Colour*	*Cost Per Page Mono*	*Frequency*
Image	25,000	£2,000	£1,300	Monthly
Woman's Way	66,166	£3,000	£1,950	Weekly
RTE Guide	170,107	£3,400	£2,050	Weekly
IT	20,283	£1,630	£1,100	Monthly
Irish Runner	10,500	£945	£670	8 p.a.
World of Irish Nursing	17,400	£1,050	£750	6 p.a.

Source: IMJ

THE DECISION

As the group were reviewing the issues above, it was clear that a go/no go decision would have to be made quickly if the goods were to be landed and in chosen outlets in time for a Spring launch. Accordingly, while the marketing sub-group was still considering its options, it was agreed with Cherokee that JBS would have exclusive rights to the Irish market for Cherokee products. In turn, JBS provided satisfactory credit references and ordered 1,700 pairs for delivery in the second half of January 1995. Grattan Boylan was landed with the job of preparing a launch, though the squabble about the 45-day test was still in full swing as Christmas approached!

APPENDIX 1: SAMPLE ADVERTISEMENT FOR ROCKERS FOR WALKERS BY CHEROKEE

8

MOFFETT ENGINEERING LTD.[1]

Elizabeth Reynolds and Seán de Burca

It was late on December 10, 1994, when Carol Moffett, Managing Director of Moffett Engineering arrived back at the office. She was looking forward to Christmas and a few days off to rest and reflect. A number of Christmas presents which she had purchased on her recent business trip were stacked on the desk beside the new list of orders and follow up contracts that she had negotiated. As she gazed at the orders, she contemplated the enormous challenge facing Moffett Engineering if they were to successfully achieve the sales growth required by the company to underwrite the investment necessary for future expansion plans.

Moffett Engineering has experienced substantial growth over the last three years. Sales of the Moffett Mounty — the company's main product line — were expected to exceed 1,000 units in 1995, with markets in almost 30 countries. Numerous opportunities existed for the Mounty, both in terms of existing and new applications.

The Mounty was a rough terrain forklift that was carried on the rear of a truck or trailer. The all-wheel-drive Mounty operated both as a rough terrain forklift and a versatile loading/offloading system in one tough package. The truck driver, single-handedly, could load the goods onto the truck at the depot, drive to the customer, and place the goods exactly where they were wanted — even over the roughest terrain. Moffett Engineering had spent several years researching the needs of the distribution industry and believed that the many applications of the Mounty could change materials handling and distribution around the world.

---

[1] This case study was prepared by Elizabeth Reynolds and Seán de Burca of University College Dublin, as a basis for class discussion rather than to illustrate either effective or ineffective handling of an administration situation.

The main challenge facing the company was to develop plans on how these applications could be further developed both in the home market and internationally. In addition, the company had to profitably harness the numerous opportunities that existed for the Moffett Mounty, both in terms of existing and new applications. They also wanted to penetrate Eastern Europe and further develop the United States market. Furthermore, the company had to devote financial and management resources to their new product, the Moffett Multi Function Tractor. Both markets were considered essential to achieve the sales volume and market share required in order to underwrite the investments necessary to become the number one truck mounted forklift and to break into the Tractor market. As the Managing Director, Carol Moffett was aware that she had a very loyal and dedicated workforce of 150 people and she was determined to ensure that their successes in the past would be continued in the future. This motivated the company to live up to its advertising copy for the Mounty as:

"THE truck mounted forklift"

Instinctively, she removed from the filing cabinet the approved 1995 marketing plan. She intended to study the plan over the next few days, and then bring together her functional heads and two directors for a one day working meeting on December 16, 1994.

COMPANY BACKGROUND

Moffett Engineering was established in the early 1940s in Clontibret, Co. Monaghan by the late Cecil Moffett as a local engineering workshop, principally engaged in designing, manufacturing and repairing agricultural machinery. In the 1950s this business developed steadily as more and more farmers were becoming increasingly mechanised. Moffett Engineering repaired and manufactured agricultural equipment for use with tractors. Furthermore, new local industries were emerging such as mushroom farming, furniture manufacturing and poultry processing. The company found a niche designing and manufacturing tailor-made equipment for these sectors.

Soon, the business built up a strong credible reputation in both the agricultural and industrial sectors and which extended well beyond the Monaghan area.

In the 1960s, Cecil Moffett realised that over the long term his business would benefit greatly by producing its own branded product which it could manufacture in small batches. He identified that there was a need for a small steel-cutting saw for use by the many small manufacturing and engineering companies that were being set up around the country. Steel-cutting saws were already available on the market costing £2,000 and this was way beyond the budget of most small engineering firms at this time. Consequently, Cecil Moffett designed and developed a steel friction cutting saw called the "Monocut" saw which he was able to sell for £300 each. This was a very successful and profitable product for Moffett Engineering and brought the company further into contact with the industrial sector. In the late 1960s, seeing the boom in construction, Moffett started to manufacture moulds for precast concrete products such as fencing posts, slats and kerb stones.

The company was ahead of its time in the Irish engineering sector having decided to make the transition from building one-off pieces of equipment to establishing its own brand product lines. The sudden death of Cecil Moffett in 1972 left 19-year-old Carol Moffett with a dilemma. Carol was the oldest in the family, studying French and Spanish at Trinity College, Dublin. Her father's death had changed her outlook. Carol knew she had a major decision to make — she could either finish her degree or return home to the family business. One afternoon as she sat on the bench overlooking the cricket pitch in Trinity, she thought long and hard about the decision she faced. She remembers now that it was an unusual sunny December afternoon, and the grounds of Trinity looked their usual splendour. She had started her essay "The role of women in South American literature", but she knew that she would never finish it. The decision was made and she returned home. Her younger brother Robert had already decided to leave school at 16 and joined forces with her. The business at that stage employed two other people.

Robert had inherited his father's flair for engineering and design. Carol Moffett did return to University years later, not as a student but as an invited guest to talk to students on the subject of entreprenuership.

NEW MANAGEMENT

Soon after taking control of the family business, Carol recognised that if the company was to grow and survive it would have to keep abreast of what was happening abroad. She had her own ideas as to the route Moffett Engineering should take. A number of trips were made to industrial trade shows around Europe. At the Hanover industrial fair, she and her brother were very impressed with a new machine that was utilising a new concept called dry mix concrete to manufacture fencing posts and slats. This dry mix method was in widespread use in Europe. Historically, these products had been made by manually mixing cement, sand and water, pouring the mix into moulds, allowing it to set and dry for 24 hours and then removing the finished products from the moulds for curing. The dry mix method meant that products could be immediately demoulded for storage and sale, thus saving valuable time with reduced labour costs. In addition, the products were stronger as less water was used in the mix. From this, Robert Moffett set about building a prototype machine for sale to the existing customer base.

Other winds of change were sweeping across Europe. Ireland's membership of the EU was beginning to have a major impact during the mid-1970s. The EU had identified Ireland as a disadvantaged economy in need of investment. In particular, the agricultural sector was identified as a potential growth sector. Farmers were given generous financial incentives to assist them to modernise and improve agricultural production. Moffett Engineering recognised a potential growth market in products related to the construction and agricultural sectors. Their new high output machine for producing precast concrete products, which they called the "Moffett Multicast", was poised to take full advantage of the improved market conditions in these sectors.

In 1978, Moffett Engineering built a new 2,500 square metres factory adjacent to the site of the old workshops. Business was expanding rapidly. The company secured its first export order to the UK. This came about opportunistically. A potential customer saw the precast concrete-making machine in action at a plant in Northern Ireland. They approached Moffett to develop a machine for them. As a result, Moffett decided to begin its export marketing effort and began participating at trade fairs in the UK. This brought them into contact with international markets for the first time. As they became more exposed to the UK market, they realised that if they improved the design and handling features of the machine they could double their sales price for each machine. In particular for large complex machines capable of producing a variety of products, and with the addition of electronic controls, prices could reach up to IR£200,000 on the European market. The UK export market flourished by making these amendments. Success in the UK gave the company the confidence to press forward into the European arena. They established contacts and contracted with a number of agents around Europe. By the end of 1983, orders were received from a number of EU countries plus Egypt, Sweden, and Austria. However, even though this business was growing, they found that it was highly cyclical and very dependent on the construction industry cycle. Since the decision-making process was very slow, both Robert and Carol believed that sustained growth and expansion of the business would not be achieved by relying on the sale of this equipment to the construction industry. They also felt that they were not getting sufficient return on the resources deployed in the company. However, the management of Moffett Engineering had learned one major lesson: developing and selling their own branded product line led to higher profits, and product quality and the ability to customise are not just necessary but essential to secure a market and ensure customer satisfaction.

As well as the management and development of these products, Carol and her younger brother Robert were continually looking for product/market opportunities that would essentially lead to wider market appeal and, in addition, could be exported in volume.

As Carol Moffett stated:

"What we need is a product that can be mass produced, and easily customised, which builds on the expertise that we have acquired in Moffett Engineering."

NEW PRODUCT RESEARCH

A detailed research programme was launched in 1984 to find new products and markets. Initially, the research focused on secondary sources of information, particularly in the area of materials handling in Europe. The company considered that this market had considerable scope for development. There were a number of reasons for this choice:

1. Increasing difficulty finding people to do manual labour.
2. Increasing cost of manual labour.
3. Pending EU legislation prohibiting manual handling of loads in excess of 30 KGs.
4. The drive for increased efficiency to bring down costs.

The company identified a number of criteria that were important to them. These criteria were specifically related to Moffett Engineering's core competencies. In particular, the company had developed specialised skills in designing hydraulic systems. Five criteria were established and considered essential by the company for any new product development. The criteria were as follows:

1. Product development should reflect their engineering design skills.
2. The product should incorporate hydraulic systems, an area of competence within the company — hence few new skills had to be learned and the risk of technical problems lessened.
3. The product should be capable of being sold and serviced through dealers/importers around the world.
4. The product should be capable of being containerised for ease of transportation.
5. The product should respond to customer needs in the materials handling category.

Company personnel set about visiting trade shows and exhibitions both in Europe and the USA examining trends in the business, looking at new products and talking to manufacturers and distributors.

THE TAIL LIFT

The first product identified that satisfied all these criteria was a tail lift.

A tail lift was developed as a solution to overcome the problem of offloading from trucks. The tail lift is a hydraulic elevating platform attached to the rear of a truck to facilitate lowering goods to the ground. It is often seen in use for deliveries to supermarkets where the goods are placed on the platform which is activated by push button control which lowers and raises the platform.

Moffett Engineering sold quite a number of tail lifts in Ireland. However, it was not a successful business venture for Moffett Engineering. They found it difficult to get enthusiastic about a product selling for £2,000 to £2,500 when they had being used to selling products for up to £200,000. They also had problems getting paid. In addition, they found that truck body builders, who were the main customers of tail lifts, were in many cases not really prepared to work with them to develop the business. However, the product did generate one real benefit. It introduced the company to transport operators for the first time.

TRANSPORT OPERATORS

Transport operators were involved in the physical movement of goods such as building products, fertilisers, and animal feeds. In particular, Agricultural Co-operatives were very prominent players in this industry and owned large transport fleets. Many of these co-operatives had purchased tail lifts from Moffett Engineering. Their largest customer was Kerry Co-operative (a large-scale agricultural co-operative selling palletised products such as seeds, fertilisers and animal feeds).

The new EU legislation had the effect of forcing people to re-examine their methods of materials handling. Additionally, in Ireland, the co-operatives were coming under huge pressure to cut costs. Traditionally, offloading of farm feeds and fertilisers was done manually by two people at the point of delivery to a specified place identified by the end user, i.e. a storage house, a shed or indeed a field. This practice had resulted in a number of compensation claims by employees for damage to their backs as a result of continuous lifting of heavy goods. In addition, this manual labour method was very slow and the trucks were often delayed for up to two hours at the delivery point. This also had the effect of reducing the productivity of each truck. When Kerry Co-operative discovered that Moffett were considering the development of a transportable forklift they revealed that they were studying the concept of speeding up the deliveries of their farm feeds and fertilisers. They stipulated that such a machine would have to be capable of lifting and carrying a two-tonne pallet across a ploughed field and yet light enough to be carried at the rear of a truck. Accordingly, the seeds of the Mounty took root. From this, Moffett Engineering built a prototype and sent it to Kerry for evaluation in the Autumn of 1985. Over the Winter months, Moffett kept a close eye on the performance of the machine and listened carefully to the drivers' feedback. Several more prototypes were built and put to the test.

THE LAUNCH OF THE MOFFETT MOUNTY

The Moffett Mounty was launched in March 1986 in the famous Ballymaloe House Hotel, County Cork, in the South of Ireland. It was a high profile launch with key representatives from the agricultural sector invited to attend. Robert Moffett, who was now the Technical Director, stated at the launch that:

> "the Moffett Mounty came about as a direct result of our research and the close collaboration with end users such as the Kerry Group. This combination provided us with a detailed understanding of the critical areas of agricultural distribution. Our product offers a fully independent discharge facility which gives operators a major opportunity to boost vehicle productivity and puts them back in control of distribution." (See Exhibits 1 and 2).

WHAT IS THE MOFFETT MOUNTY — HOW DOES IT WORK?

The three-wheeled Mounty is a lightweight forklift capable of being transported on the rear of most trucks or trailers. It is raised and lowered from the trailer by means of its own hydraulic power. A mounting kit, which includes support brackets for the front wheels of the forklift, is welded or bolted to the trailer or flat bed truck. The machine is secured in position by means of two chains. The front tyres of the forklift act as shock absorbers ensuring that very little shock is felt by the machine during transit. The Mounty is powered by a diesel engine which in turn powers the hydraulics. The machine can be detached from the stowage position in less than one minute and reattached in the same time. It has power steering and finger tip control from the driver's seat, making it very operator-friendly.

Principally, the Mounty executes all the functions of a conventional forklift — lifting and carrying loads, loading, offloading vehicles/stacking and positioning of goods. In addition, the Mounty has the manoeuvrability to work in the tightest, most congested areas by means of the third rotating wheel at the rear. A drive motor fitted to each wheel enables the machine to operate in most types of terrain.

Although the Moffett Mounty is a forklift, it does not compete with conventional forklifts, which are normally used in warehouses. Rough terrain forklifts for use on farms or on building sites are very large and expensive. The Mounty's real competitor is the crane. However, it can differentiate itself substantially from a crane. Unlike a crane, the Mounty is not permanently attached to the truck or trailer. The Mounty can cross rough terrain, whereas the crane and truck must remain on hard standing. The Mounty does not take up load space, whereas some cranes do. Centre-mounted cranes in particular restrict the type of load that can be carried. The Mounty can service several trucks whereas the crane can only service its own truck. Cranes are restricted to working within a small radius of the vehicle whereas the Mounty can travel anywhere on site. Similarly, as the mounting kits are relatively inexpensive, several trailers in a fleet can be adapted for use with the Mounty thus improving flexibility. A major difference between the two is that the Mounty can deliver into buildings and service curtainsiders and covered trucks. The Mounty uses less fuel than a crane and maintenance can be done on the Mounty without tying up the truck. A higher level of competence is required to operate a crane, due in principle to the damage that could be done, for example, to overhead power lines.

The Mounty is available in ten basic models (see Exhibit 3) with a maximum carrying capacity of 2.7 tons for the largest machine. These machines have being developed for different applications and various markets ranging from agricultural products, building materials to the fire service. New applications are constantly being discovered and this process is aided by Moffett's willingness to customise the product, for example, the addition of clamps, grabs or special forks. The machine is also very reliable, and is guaranteed for one year. It requires little maintenance. Safety features such as a roll bar are standard.

MOFFETT MOUNTY — BENEFITS

As the Mounty puts the transport operator in control, the Mounty offers operators the following benefits:

1. They can schedule their own loading/offloading schedules as there is no waiting around for offloading assistance.
2. They can perform out of hours deliveries.
3. They can achieve a quicker turnaround. As a result they can do more deliveries, with less vehicles, in less time, at lower cost.
4. Collections are possible as well as deliveries.
5. In addition, the final customer is provided with a better service as goods delivered to them can be placed exactly where they are required.
6. The addition of a Mounty to a fleet ensures better scheduling, less manpower, less capital investment trucks, and ultimately lower delivery costs.
7. It reduces product damage as it eliminated manual handling. This reduces the risk of injuries to operatives, which should eventually result in lower insurance premiums.

MARKET POTENTIAL

The market potential in each country has proved difficult to calculate. The market is in an early development phase and is at this stage relatively small and immature. This makes estimating the market potential difficult since it is constantly evolving. Moffett Engineering believe that ability to achieve sales is determined more by its own marketing capability and that of its competitors than any limitation caused by the potential of the market. The Mounty sales history is shown in Table 1.

TABLE 1: MOFFETT MOUNTY SALES HISTORY — 1986-94

Years	*1986*	*1988*	*1990*	*1991*	*1992*	*1993*	*1994*
Sales Units	14	119	120	236	250	405	725

In 1986, when the Moffett Mounty was first introduced, 14 units were sold to the agricultural sector. Sales have increased steadily to 725 machines by the end of 1994. The Moffett Mounty was being exported to almost 30 countries and was being utilised in a number of different applications. Carol Moffett believed that the company had only touched the tip of the iceberg in terms of potential and had a very bright future ahead. She was already well on the way of dominating this niche of the materials handling sectors world-wide. The company plan for growth was based on increasing sales to over 1,500 machines by the end of 1996 to generate a market share of 50 per cent world-wide (see Exhibit 4).

MARKETING OBJECTIVES AND STRATEGY

Moffett Engineering outlined their marketing objectives as follows:

- To establish the Moffett Mounty as the number one truck mounted forklift in the world.
- To develop a clear identity and brand name for the Moffett Mounty world-wide.
- To ensure that Moffett Engineering Ltd. established an international sales and distribution network second to none.

- To build on and enhance its existing reputation as an innovative manufacturer of materials handling equipment and to achieve this on a selective global scale.
- To achieve the sales projections as outlined in Exhibit 4 over the next five years.
- To identify further opportunities in the market place through its close contact with key customers and distributors and to keep ahead of future developments in the material handling area, e.g. to develop attachments for the Mounty thus further enhancing its marketability.
- To develop and implement a total support package including training and documentation to the sales and distribution network.
- To become a low-cost producer capable of keeping competitors at bay.

To achieve the above objectives the company devised strategies with respect to products, promotions, customers, service levels, training and development and management support as follows:

Products

- Through a heavy emphasis on design to provide its customers with "superior" products to those of its competitors.
- To constantly listen to and monitor customer comment and feedback.

Marketing

- To create the Moffett Mounty as an internationally known and respected brand name with a clear corporate identity for Moffett Engineering Ltd.

Customers

- To identify in each industry the early adopters, to target these adopters and use them as a basis for developing and expanding the market in each country. In addition, to target specific industries such as brewing, where the cost benefit ratios are attractive, or the Fire service, which needs to reduce manual handling.

Service
Initially this means supplying promptly on placement of order. Also, it involves investing in service backup. This backup consists of:

- Training dealers to be responsive and professional in their approach.
- Producing documentation on the machine.
- Setting up dealer and service training schools.
- Stocking and supplying spare parts.
- Giving technical support as required.

Training and Development

- To ensure all staff in all areas are trained to a high level in use of technology, marketing/sales techniques, customer service and quality management, enabling the company to be perceived a responsive, market-led manufacturer of high quality products.

Management Support

- To ensure that management team support to the distributors/dealers and sales representatives is sustained at a high level.

PROMOTION

Moffett Engineering's long-term strategy for the Mounty was to become the number one truck mounted forklift in the world. Jacinta McMahon, the Marketing Administrator, summarised the company's position succinctly:

> "the challenge is to create the Moffett Mounty as an internationally known and respected brand name with a clear corporate identity."

Marketing activity focused on adopters, who were targeted for use as endorsers of the Mounty for use in promotional videos, brochures, public relations and demonstrations activity.

Sean Quinn (Quarries) Ltd. in Northern Ireland endorsed the Moffett Mounty as a major tool vital to customer relations:

> "getting cement to where it is required, on time, with the packaging undamaged, is vital. As part of our service we can offload deliveries on site or into the merchant's store using the Moffett Mounty forklift" (*World Cement*, November, 1989).

Philip Hastings in the *Financial Times* (February 22, 1990) endorsed the Moffett Mounty as a way to avoid traffic congestion by using night time deliveries.

Roofing Contractor Peter Hunt endorsed the Moffett Mounty because he believed it gave him the competitive edge by offering an independent forklift delivery service.

Brampton Brick, the second largest clay brick producer in Canada, uses the Moffett Mounty. Mike Burns, who runs Brampton's transport company believes that:

> "the Mounty gives greater service than other forklifts because of its reliable performance on rough terrain" (*Equipment Journal*, December 20, 1990).

Brian Phillpot, Commercial Director of Ischebeck Titan, a large UK-based construction company, said about the new four way Moffett Mounty:

> "basically Mounty is three forklifts in one, a normal counterbalance forklift, a reach truck and a side loader with rough terrain capability ideal for yard handling and vehicle loading" (*Timber Trade Journal*, October 29, 1994).

Essex County Fire and Rescue Service believe that:

> "the Moffett Mounty will make a vital contribution to the reduction of injuries caused by lifting heavy objects and, as such, it will play an important role in the health and safety of fire fighters" (*Fire Magazine,* June 1994).

Industrial trade shows were used to illustrate both how the product worked and to provide information on cost efficiencies, operational issues, dealers, after-sales services, and to form a potential list of contact companies. Promotional literature included specialist booklets outlining how *the* Moffett Mounty could be used to its full potential. This booklet also provided information on cost savings and operational efficiencies endorsed by Mounty users all around the world. In the UK and Europe, a Moffett Mounty Mobile Exhibition display unit was used at trade shows and in company demonstrations.

Moffett Engineering intends to publish the first edition of a bi-annual publication, called "Move It", which will be circulated to dealers and customers world-wide. It will contain information on new applications, developments in the company, country profiles and an introduction to some of the key personnel at the company.

In 1992, IR£280,000 was spent on promotional activity. This had increased to IR£450,000 by the end of 1994. Promotional investment in the future was budgeted to increase in accordance with sales increases.

PRICING

Prices were set by Moffett Engineering. They stipulated the retail price with all their dealers world-wide. Mounty machines ranged in price from IR£11,500 for their 1.2 tonne model to IR£29,000 for their top of the range 2.7 tonne model. Prices included the mounting bracket for the truck.

DISTRIBUTION

Moffett distributed to over 30 countries around the world. With the exception of the UK, all markets were served by dealers who covered a pre-agreed territory. Most agents were initially introduced to Moffett at trade fairs. The company used a number of criteria for choosing a dealer:

1. They should already be established in the materials handling business, and be financially sound.
2. They should be prepared to dedicate one salesperson to the Mounty.
3. They should buy at least 2 units for stock.

4. They should be prepared to carry out demonstrations.

Moffett Engineering provided dealers with sales manuals, spare parts manuals, operators manuals, mounting kit manuals, videos and after-sales service training. They also had regular contact to ensure their customer care and after sales policy was understood and implemented by their dealers. Targets, prices and territory were agreed with dealers in advance of their appointment. The dealers were visited periodically and were encouraged to bring potential customers to Ireland. Every year the company held dealer meetings where up to 70 dealers attended. Moffett Engineering felt that this was a useful method of disseminating information, building team spirit and motivating people. In the UK Moffett had its own sales team selling on a commission basis and did not operate a dealer network.

RESEARCH AND DEVELOPMENT

Investment in research and development stood at 5 per cent of annual turnover. Research involved identifying new applications and designing machines to suit each new application. Models were continually upgraded based on customer feedback. Carol Moffett states the case as follows:

> "No model stands still at Moffett — we are always looking at ways to improve our machines as well as producing them in a more cost effective manner without sacrificing quality and reliability."

Product design was based on two principles — customer requirements and identification of potential new uses. In addition, competitive products were constantly examined and their performance analysed. Moffett Engineering paid particular attention to the applications competitors were targeting. Critical to the design of the Mounty was matching it to the size and dimensions of the truck to which it was to be attached. Each customer supplied information to Moffett Engineering about the length, width, axle loads and the loadspace that the truck could carry. A drawing was produced on AutoCAD showing the Mounty fitted to the rear of the truck and its effect on loadspace and on the axle loading of the truck. Martin McVicar, Design Engineer, believed this was a critical part of the design process as it ensured that the customer saw exactly what he was getting.

Moffett Engineering formed a new Research and Development company in 1991. This company held the patents to several design features on the Moffett Mounty. All research and development at Moffett Engineering was carried out in this new research company in Clontibret. The main objective for designers was to ensure optimal performance and stability at a minimal weight. Attachments were also designed and tested. Attempts were made to ensure as much commonality of components as possible across the range.

ASSEMBLY

The Moffett Mounty was manufactured in Ireland at their two factories in Clontibret and a third factory was acquired in late 1993 in Dundalk. The components for the machines were manufactured in Dundalk. The assembly of the machine took place on a production line in Clontibret. Assembly involved four basic steps: fabrication, painting, assembly, and testing. A critical part of assembly was the testing procedures.

TESTING

Testing was done during assembly. The most essential part of the machine — the hydraulic system — was tested by filtering out any potential dirt or grime to a 5-micron level to ensure no particles were left in the system. All components were individually tested before assembly. On completion each machine was given a full operational check.

REGULATORY COMPLIANCE

As a European product, the machine had to comply with directive 86/663/EC. When mounted on a truck the product had to comply with the directive 85/3/EC. All the components complied with the individual directives for each individual part. Where possible patent protection was obtained for unique design features of the Moffett Mounty. Trucks had to carry a maximum legal weight which had to be balanced between the front and back axle. The Moffett Mounty had to comply with these conditions while maximising the loadspace (amount of material they can carry) after taking the weight of the Moffett Mounty into consideration.

APPLICATIONS

Initially designed for agricultural use, the Moffett Mounty had now evolved to serve numerous applications. There were six major sectors where applications had been developed. These were agricultural supplies, horticultural supplies, poultry, building products, distribution and fire service. Other miscellaneous uses had also emerged such as waste materials handling, food, beverages, fuel, and erecting marquees (see Exhibit 5). Carol Moffett believed that the number of applications was only limited by the imagination of the sales people and their ability to communicate the benefits of the Mounty system.

DEVELOPING NEW APPLICATIONS

Sources for the development of new applications arose from a number of areas. These include feedback from end users and dealers or observing niches where Moffett Engineering believed a Mounty could be used. A significant amount of developmental work was carried out with local Irish and UK companies who specified the conditions and specifications. Moffett felt that there were tremendous benefits in getting close to the customer.

Moffett Engineering believed that their success in developing new applications stemmed from the consistent use of the following methodology. They researched a sector of the market where they believed there were benefits to be gained from using the Mounty. Specifically they did the following:

1. Established facts and figures to support their belief in the benefit of the Mounty in this sector.

2. Found a customer who was willing to try the machine, sometimes by way of a rental if he or she were not prepared to invest the capital.

3. Worked closely with the customer and their drivers to ensure that the Mounty was used to its maximum potential.
4. Organised mailings, trade shows and public relations activities in this sector.
5. Invited their "guinea pig" customers to act as testimonials.

The company had gone for a very targeted approach breaking the market into sectors and had encouraged their dealers to adopt this approach.

DEVELOPING THE LIVE POULTRY MOUNTY

The success of the Moffett Mounty in the poultry industry illustrated how new applications and machines had developed. Barry McEntee, Managing Director of Monaghan Poultry Products, approached Moffett Engineering about developing a Mounty for use in his live poultry collection. Poultry houses had low access doors with narrow aisles. They had deep litter on the floor which made driving conditions difficult. The poultry containers had an extended load centre being 2.4 metres long, 1.2 metres wide and weighing about 1 tonne, which had to be handled with extreme care. Moffett Engineering developed its M2275 model capable of meeting these parameters. It had a low mast, enabling it to go right through the low doors into the poultry houses. With its three-wheel configuration, it could turn within its own radius making it highly manoeuvrable in confined spaces.

The M2275 Model was equipped with long forks to handle the 8 foot containers. A special tread tyre was fitted to cater for the wet and deep litter. As poultry collection is normally done at night time, special blue lights were fitted to ensure that the poultry could not see the machine in the dark. After Monaghan Poultry Products adopted the Mounty, their transport operating costs reduced from 12 per cent to 3 per cent. As a result of this success Moffett Engineering began to develop this application internationally, with permission from Monaghan Poultry Products to show the machine in operation in their premises. Moffett Engineering identified that the transportation, safety and handling issues of the poultry industry in Ireland were roughly the same all over the world.

A similar process was used for the development of many other applications and a strong working relationship was formed with the lead customer to develop the application to its maximum potential.

AFTER-SALES SERVICE AND BACKUP

After-sales service was controlled in Ireland and the UK by Moffett Engineering. In the other markets this was the responsibility of their dealers. Dealers were trained extensively on the installation of trailer mounting kits and machine maintenance. Dealers were encouraged to carry parts in stock. In addition, the company guaranteed that any spare part would be delivered on a next day basis to a dealer or direct to the customer throughout Europe and the USA. Spare parts supply to the rest of the world was guaranteed within two to three days.

COMPETITORS

The management of Moffett Engineering did not consider themselves in the forklift business per se, competing with forklift companies such as Nissan, Yale or Komatsu. They believed that the Mounty competed with other offloading methods more than other brands of truck mounted forklifts. Specifically, the Mounty competed with the following offloading methods:

1. Truck-mounted cranes
2. Forklifts at the point of delivery
3. Manual offloading
4. Tail lifts
5. Other makes of truck-mounted forklifts.

Cranes

Cranes were considered by Moffett to be direct competitors in the materials offloading handling niche market. The differences between cranes and the Mounty have been outlined earlier.

Predominantly, they were used in the heavy building products and lumber sector to offload heavy products. The crane was always attached permanently to the truck and was operated by the driver. The crane market was highly developed in Europe, and for many customers was the automatic choice as an offloading device. Over 4,000 cranes were sold annually in Britain, 5,000 in Germany and just over 4,000 in France. Moffett Engineering believed that there was an opportunity to convert some crane users to Mounty users, as in many instances it was a better alternative than the crane since it offered more flexibility.

Truck-mounted Forklifts

Three competitors manufactured mounted forklifts in Europe: Kooi-aap, Audureau and Schmidt. In the American market, there were two main competitors, Princeton and Spyder, and finally Brouwer of Canada. Estimated market share is given in Exhibit 6.

Kooi-aap

Kooi-aap was based in the Netherlands. They were established in 1974 and employed 100 people in their family run business. They produced 23 models of machines. They had concentrated on the light duty 1 tonne and 1.5 tonne single wheel drive end of the market, i.e. the consumer goods segment. The major differences between the Moffett Mounty and the Kooi-aap product were in relation to the drive and mast. The Kooi-aap had telescopic forks rather than the travelling mast arrangement of the Moffett Mounty. Moffett Engineering believed that telescopic forks were a major weakness. The Kooi-aap product was generally more expensive than the Mounty. They had exported mainly to Belgium, Germany, and the UK and were viewed as a serious competitor to Moffett Engineering.

Audureau

This French company had manufactured rough terrain forklifts for over 10 years. Four years ago they moved into the truck-mounted forklift business, concentrating solely on the heavy duty end of the market with a 1.5 tonne and 2.0 tonne machine. Their prices were at least 10 per cent below the Moffett Mounty, and their technical specifications were also lower than the Mounty. Originally, they concentrated on the French market, but they had recently appointed an agent in Quebec in Canada. Their Cab2000 was their leading product line aimed primarily at agricultural use.

Schmidt
Schmidt was a relatively small manufacturer and supplied the German market only. They produced only one machine, a 1 tonne which was targeted at the beverage industry. Moffett Engineering believed they should have a machine in this category. Their product was a little more expensive than the Moffett Mounty. They did not export.

Princeton
This company was a subsidiary of a major multinational company, Teledyne Inc. They were based in Columbus, Ohio, with 100 employees. Up to 1992, they concentrated their sales in the peat, bog and turf areas with a 2 wheel drive machine. They called their machine "Piggyback".

As a reaction to the Mounty which had a higher specification, they introduced for the first time a three-wheel-drive model. Six models were available with a range of engines in either gas or diesel. They had a number of attachments that could be used with the machine depending on the customer's requirements. This machine was 400 kilograms heavier than the Mounty and 30 centimetres longer when carried at the rear of the truck. It did not have conventional steering and controls and was considered by many to be less operator friendly. When the Mounty appeared on the market, they immediately reduced their prices to a few per cent below the Mounty.

Spyder
This was the cheapest machine on the market. It concentrated on the sod and turf market and was considered to have a lower technical specification. Four models were available. The main selling feature was its light weight with the capability of handling up to 3,000 KGs. They were priced lower than the Mounty.

Brouwer
They produced a limited range of products aimed mainly at the sod sector. Their prices were similar to the Mounty. They were not viewed as a serious competitor.

INTRODUCTION TO THE MAIN MARKETS

Moffett Engineering exported mainly to the UK, USA, Canada, Mexico, Colombia, Chile, Australia, New Zealand, Malaysia, Thailand, South Africa, Egypt, Portugal, Spain, France, Austria, Poland, Germany, Denmark, Belgium and The Netherlands. Three markets had been identified as key to the achievement of their strategic plan: the UK, USA and Germany.

UK

This was still Moffett's largest market and a significant contributor to their overall sales. The company attended over fifteen trade shows annually and had a comprehensive and sustained public relations programme. Five applications had been targeted in this market. An important application was live poultry as over 1,069,000 tonnes of poultry meat were processed annually in Britain. This market was 13 times bigger than the Irish market.

The construction industry accounted for 60 per cent of Moffett sales in the UK. To increase market penetration in this sector the new Mounty Four-Way was developed to handle long-length products such as pipes, timber, roofing sheets and boards. The machine could be converted into a side loader in 30 seconds. While still retaining full steering control all wheels could turn through 90 degrees which allowed the Mounty to travel sideways. The Four-Way Mounty also had a reach height of 3.04 metres, which allowed access to high racking systems.

The third area of focus centred on agricultural products such as feeds, fertilisers, compost, slats and storage tanks. This was an area where Moffett Engineering had begun in Ireland and had already achieved considerable success.

The fourth area was fire and rescue operations. This was a new area for Moffett. This included the loading and offloading of pallets of foam for firefighting and the removal of dangerous chemicals. It also involved the removal of obstructions to allow fire engines the closest possible access to the scene of the incident. The Mounty was used for assisting in the removal of damaged vehicles from road traffic accidents. In addition, it was also of enormous benefit in carrying the firefighters own equipment, thus reducing manual handling and consequent risk of injury to personnel.

Another major application targeted market was the Bottled Gas sector. These companies used the Mounty to offload pallets of gas cylinders at customer's premises. Again the risk of injury to personnel was reduced and the customers got a better service.

In 1990, Moffett Engineering decided to set up a UK sales company, Moffett Sales and Service Limited. The company purchased a 6,000 square foot premises adjacent to the motorway network in Rotherham, South Yorkshire which it purchased in 1991. Initially two Irish employees were relocated to this office to work in sales, after sales service and spare parts.

Eight people were eventually employed — five in sales, and three in service and administrative support. Sales meetings were held every month and a specific sector was chosen for discussion at each meeting. A concerted effort was made to target that particular sector by every member of the team in the forthcoming month. Application videos specific to that sector were made and sent to target companies. Press releases were prepared and sent to the relevant trade magazines. The Moffett Mounty Mobile Exhibition display unit was used extensively at trade shows and for in-company demonstrations. A limited amount of advertising in targeted trade media was placed. Carol Moffett had taken specific responsibility for the UK market and spent much of her time there. Progress was slow at the beginning as the recession was in full swing. It was difficult getting across to companies who were mostly suffering a major slowdown.

USA

Moffett first entered the US market in 1988. They appointed a dealer in Atlanta who had previously carried the Princeton line and who was well known in materials handling. Their initial market entry was low key to assess the opportunities for the Mounty in the Atlanta region. They particularly wanted to test the potential competitive reaction. However, in January 1989 the dealership was cancelled as sales were being generated all over the United States without the necessary service and training backup that was essential for Moffett to succeed in this highly competitive market. A new dealer, Dunbar (now Cargotec), based in Ohio was appointed. Historically, Dunbar manufactured rolling base cranes. However, they identified the Moffett Mounty as a complementary product for their range. They developed the truck-mounted forklift business from scratch and by 1993 held a 40 per cent share of the building material market in the USA. Cargotec have intentions to further develop this market over the next five years. The main applications that had been targeted for expansion were building materials and the lumber industry. Cranes had traditionally been used in this sector but they saw cranes sales decrease as the Mounty got established. It was their long-term plan to move into other applications once these initial markets had been well established.

Germany

Gruenewald GmbH, Saarbruecken, was the main dealer in Germany. Timber, poultry, gas companies, fire authorities, agriculture and the engineering sector were the main applications targeted for development.

ORGANISATIONAL STRUCTURE

Moffett Engineering employed 150 between their two factories at Clontibret and Dundalk. In addition eight people were employed in the UK. The organisation is headed up by Carol Moffett, the Managing Director. She has won many awards for her management and business abilities including the "Veuve Clicquot Businesswoman of the Year" award and The Allied Irish Bank's "Exporter of the Year" award. There were two other directors — Operations and Technical — who formed the board of the company. The organisation was divided into seven functional areas: marketing/sales, administration, finance, manufacturing, materials, engineering and research and development. Each of these areas had a functional head who reported directly to the Managing Director and Production Director.

TIME TO REFLECT

As Carol Moffett sat in her Clontibret office, she reviewed the final launch plan for their new exciting product which had taken over two years to develop — the new Moffett Multi Function Tractor. She was quietly optimistic and excited about this new product. However, she was well aware of the major challenges that lay ahead. Numerous opportunities existed for the Moffett Mounty, both in terms of existing and new applications. The company also wanted to penetrate Eastern Europe and further develop the United States market. In addition, the new Moffett Multi Function Tractor would take up valuable resources both in terms of finance and management time if it was to succeed. Both markets were considered essential to achieve the sales volume and market share required in order to underwrite the investment necessary to become the number one truck-mounted forklift and to break into the tractor market. In addition, she had just signed a cheque for all staff to attend a customer care workshop in early January 1995 to ensure that their total commitment to the customer would continue. She looked at her watch and decided it was time to leave. As she walked to her car with the plans in her briefcase to get a flight to the UK office, she knew that December 16 was the day for her and the other company directors to review the plans which they had agreed and worked on for months. The future of Moffett Engineering depended on their success.

Suggested Readings

Ayal, I. and Zif, J. (1979): "Market Expansion Strategies in Multinational Marketing", *Journal of Marketing*, 43: 84-94.

Cheron, E.J. and Kleinschmidt E.J. (1985): "A Review of Industrial Market Segmentation Research", *International Journal of Research in Marketing*, 2: 101-115.

Johanson, J. and Vahlne, J.E. (1977): "The Internationalisation Process of the Firm — Model of Knowledge Development and Increasing Foreign Marketing Commitments", *Journal of International Business Studies*, 8(1): 22-30.

Hallen, L. and Weidersheim-Paul, F. (1983): "The Evolution of Psychic Distance in Overseas Markets Entry Strategies", *Journal of International Business Studies*, 3: 33-50.

Kumar, V., Stam, A. and Joachinsthaler, E.A. (1994): "An Integrative Multicriteria Approach to Identifying Potential Foreign Markets", *Journal of International Marketing*, 2(1): 29-52.

Plank, R.E. (1985): "A Critical Review of Industrial Market Segmentation", *Industrial Marketing Management*, 14, May: 79-91.

Weidersheim-Paul, F., Olson, H.C. and Welch, L. (1978): "Pre-export Activity: The First Step in Internationalisation", *Journal of International Business Studies*, 9(1): 47-58.

EXHIBIT 1: THE MOFFETT MOUNTY

EXHIBIT 2: THE MOFFETT MOUNTY IN ACTION

EXHIBIT 3: MOFFETT MOUNTY MODELS — MACHINE SPECIFICATIONS

Model	*Capacity*	*Load Centre*
M1501	1500 KG	500mm
M1601 L.P.	1600 KG	500mm
M1603 L.P.	1600 KG	500mm
M2003	2000 KG	500mm
M2403 W	2400 KG	500mm
M2403 N	2400 KG	500mm
M2275	2275 KG	500mm
M2275(Special)	2275 KF	500mm
M2703 N	2700 KG	500mm
M2703 W	2700 KG	500mm
M2703 4W	2700 KG	500mm
M2003 4W	2000 KG	500mm

EXHIBIT 4: SALES PROJECTIONS — UNITS 1995-2000

Year	*1995*	*1996*	*1997*	*1998*	*2000*
Total Market	2,350	3,000	3,700	4,600	5,500
Moffett -Units	1,000	1,300	1,700	2,200	2,750
Moffett -Share	42.2%	43.3%	45.9%	47.8%	50%

EXHIBIT 5: MARKET APPLICATIONS

The following is only a partial list of materials the All Wheel Drive Moffett Mounty is handling around the world today.

Building Products
- Brick
- Block
- Paving Stones
- Roof Tiles, Slates
- Roof Sheets
- Cement, Plaster
- Flooring Beams
- Hollow Core Slabs
- Plasterboard
- Timber
- Pipes — Clay/Concrete
- Precast Concrete Products
- Scaffolding

Utility Equipment
- Transformers
- Cable Reels
- Utility Stores

Food and Beverage
- Bottled Water
- Beer — Kegs/bottles in crates
- Soft drinks
- Sugar
- Canned Foods
- Potatoes
- Fruit and Vegetables

Fuel
- Bottled Gases

Prefabricated Buildings
Ceramic Tiles
Glass
Agricultural Products
Farm Buildings — Components
Storage Tanks — Components
Flooring Slats
Fertiliser — 50 Kg bags on pallets
Fertiliser —500 Kg or 1000 Kg bags
Animal Feed — Bags on pallets
Animal Feed — Slings of bags
Seed
Compost
Straw Bales
Live Poultry
Landscape Materials
Earthenware Pots
Sod
Peat
Decorative Stone
Trees/Shrubs
Coal
Peat Briquettes
Fire Wood
Miscellaneous
Grandstands
Parts and Consumables
Express Parcel Deliveries
Night Time Deliveries
Vaults
Clay Pigeons
Safes
Fridges/Freezers
Earthenware Pots
Low Ground Pressure Applications
Tents
Exhibition displays

EXHIBIT 6: WORLD-WIDE ESTIMATED MARKET SHARE OF ROUGH TERRAIN MOUNTED FORKLIFTS, 1992

Company	*Units*	*Market Share*
Moffett Mounty	250	21.2%
Kooi-aap	350	29.7%
Audureaq	100	8.5%
Princeton	300	25.5%
Spyder	100	8.5%
Brouwer	75	6.6%
Total Market	1,175	100%

Teaching Notes

Teaching notes for A CASE STUDIES IN MARKETING are available free of charge to lecturers who adopt the text for their courses.

For further information, contact:
Marketing Department, Oak Tree Press
Merrion Building, Lower Merrion Street
Dublin 2
Tel: (01) 676-1600
Fax: (01) 676-1644